SEX, PUBERTY

AND ALL THAT STUFF

For Joss and Cleo, with love.

First edition for the United States and
Canada published in 2004 by Barron's
Educational Series, Inc.
First hardcover edition published in 2004 by
Franklin Watts,
338 Euston Road, London, NW1 3BH
Designed by Matthew Lilly
Illustrated by Jan McCafferty

ISBN-13: 978-0-7641-2992-6
ISBN-10: 0-7641-2992-9
Library of Congress Catalog Card
No.: 2004102078

Created for Franklin Watts by

two's COMPANY

Copyright © Two's Company 2004

Franklin Watts
338 Euston Road, London, NW1 3BH

Franklin Watts Australia
45–51 Huntley Street
Alexandria NSW 2015

Printed by South China
Printing Co. Ltd., Dongguan, China
February 2015
19 18 17 16 15

SEX,

PUBERTY

AND ALL
THAT
STUFF

▶ A GUIDE TO GROWING UP

BY
JACQUI BAILEY

BARRON'S

True or False?

You can't get pregnant if you have sex standing up.

Find out in chapter 7

You can't use a tampon if you are a virgin.

Find out in chapter 4

Gender is another word for sex.

Find out in chapter 1

Exercise makes you feel happy.

Find out in chapter 5

Sperm is made in the penis.

Find out in chapter 3

You can catch AIDS from toilet seats.

Find out in chapter 8

Having sex clears up pimples on your skin.

Find out in chapter 6

Girls grow more quickly than boys.

Find out in chapter 2

You have to be 16 or over to buy condoms.

Find out in chapter 8

Contents

WHY DO I NEED TO KNOW THIS STUFF?

BECAUSE IT'S ALL ABOUT YOU! IT'S ABOUT YOUR BODY AND THE WAYS in which it will change as you grow older. It's about the effect these changes can have on your life, your feelings and your future. It's about growing up.

▶ **GROWING UP** is exciting, but it can be scary, too. You will want (and will get) more freedom to make your own decisions about your life. But new freedoms bring new responsibilities.

The decisions you make, and the actions you take, affect your family, friends and other people around you. But most of all, they affect you. Discovering how to make the right kind of choices for yourself and your life is what growing up is all about.

▶ **MAKING DECISIONS** isn't always easy. Even simple choices — how you style your hair, what clothes you wear, what music you like — can bring you into conflict with those around you.

Sometimes it's hard to choose between what you want for yourself and what other people (parents, teachers, friends) want for you.

And sometimes you just don't know what you want.

That's okay. Growing up is also about finding out who you are. You don't have to have all of the answers right away. If you're not sure how you feel about something, then just wait a while until you are. There's no rush. One thing you do have is plenty of time.

SO HOW WILL this book help? Well, first of all it gives you lots of information about how your body physically changes as you grow from a child to an adult — on the inside as well as on the outside.

Some of these changes are the same whether you're a boy or a girl, and some are different. In both cases they are pretty dramatic.

Understanding how and why your body is changing will make it a lot less worrying and confusing. And knowing that everyone goes through similar changes will give you more confidence in yourself and in how you deal with others.

CHECK IT OUT
Growing up can make you feel —
angry ... excited ... grumpy ... happy ...
shy ... sure of yourself ... embarrassed ...
bold ... anxious ... full of energy ... sad ...
sentimental ... lonely ... restless ...
argumentative ... and sometimes wonderful.

▶ **BUT IT ISN'T ONLY** your body that changes. Your feelings and emotions, the things you're interested in, and the things you want, will change too. In fact, sometimes they'll change so often and so much, you won't know if you are coming or going!

So, second, this book will help you to understand that the kinds of feelings, fears and worries you might go through are completely normal. You are not the only one to have them — everyone else does, too.

▶ **WHY IS IT HAPPENING** to you? Well, basically it's all because of sex! All of these changes take place for just one reason — to make your body sexually mature * so that you can make babies (or "reproduce," if you're a scientist).

The problem with this is that our bodies and our emotions don't develop at quite the same speed. We become physically able to have babies long before we are emotionally ready to have them. And believe me, having a baby is the BIGGEST responsibility you will ever face in your life. So it's well worth making sure that it is something you really want to do, rather than something you've stumbled into.

So third, this book tells you a lot of stuff about sex — about sexual feelings and fantasies, about the differences between love and sex, and what happens when two people "make love" (have sexual intercourse).

> * **Mature** is another way of saying that something has finished growing or is fully developed. When wine is mature it's ready to be drunk. When cheese matures it's ready for eating. When people mature they are adults.

It explains how babies are made, and what happens during pregnancy and birth. And it describes the ways in which you can protect yourself and others from an unwanted pregnancy or a sexually transmitted disease. It also gives you a list of useful organizations to contact if you need more specific help.

▶ **SO WHY IS SEX** such a big deal? Well, mostly because it plays a hugely important part in our lives. Just think what the word "sex" means, for a start:

1 If someone asks what sex you are, they are asking about your gender. They want to know if you are male (a boy) or female (a girl). Most living things belong to one or other of these two groups *, so even before you know the word exists, sex is a pretty big part of who you are.

2 "Having sex" is also shorthand for having sexual intercourse. This is the way that humans reproduce — so without sex none of us would be here. Which is a pretty impressive thought just on its own!

3 Then there's "sex drive," which is the automatic built-in desire or need that we have to get really close to another person. To share our thoughts and feelings with them and often to have some kind of sexual relationship with them.

Birds and Bees

All living things reproduce in some way, whether they're a bird, a bug, or a beech tree — and many of them use sex to do it! Sexual reproduction happens when a male sex cell and a female sex cell join together. (Cells are the tiny bits of matter from which all living things are made.) Sexual reproduction is how most plants make seeds, how some animals lay eggs, and how other animals, like us, give birth to live young.

* **Some living things** don't need to be male or female; they can reproduce entirely on their own. Bacteria, for example, just divide themselves in two. And a few creatures, such as earthworms, are both sexes at once!

It's our sex drive that draws or attracts us to other people, and makes us want to be attractive to them. How we look, what we wear, and how we behave have a lot to do with our sex drive, which means that sex can affect our lives in ways that we aren't even aware of.

▶ **IN FACT, SEX CAN BE** a lot of different things. It can be fun and romance, excitement and pleasure, love and desire. It can be caring and companionship, and making babies.

But, unfortunately, it can also be hurtful and bullying, and dangerous to our health and well-being.

Sex is a very powerful thing, but in itself it is neither good nor bad. It's what we do with it that counts.

Which is why you need to know what sex is and how it can affect you, so you can understand your own sexual feelings and wants (when you have them), and decide how you're going to deal with them — and with other people's.

TALKING ABOUT SEX . . .

Some people find it very difficult or embarrassing to talk about sex (and if adults are embarrassed by it, then often young people are too). Sometimes it's because they don't know much about it and don't want to seem stupid. And sometimes it's because they feel that sex is a very private and personal thing and they don't want to talk about it to anyone.

Don't try to force people into telling you things if they don't want to, but don't let their embarrassment (or yours) stop you from asking someone else.

So Dad, you and Mom only had sex once, right?

Hey, have you heard the one about ...

WORDS, WORDS, WORDS

People often make jokes about sex, or use crude words when they talk about it. Sometimes this is because they don't know the correct words, or they feel so awkward when they talk about sex that they have to make a joke to hide their embarrassment. Sometimes people use crude words or jokes because they think it makes them seem smart or grown up.

It is natural to be curious about crude words and jokes. It's all part of finding out about sex. But be aware that they can make people feel very upset or angry. Many people think that it's wrong to make fun of sex and the sexual parts of our bodies. So respect other people's feelings and keep the crude words and jokes between your friends and yourself.

▶ **SO WILL THIS BOOK** solve all your problems? Well, no. It won't. No book could. It can only give you advice and information, and hopefully help you to find your own way through the growing-up maze.

We all face much the same challenges when we are growing up, but because each of us is unique we deal with them in different ways. So use this book as a guide, but keep adding to your store of information along the way.

You can get all kinds of useful information from books, magazines, the radio, television, the Internet, and your friends. Remember, though, that not everything you read or hear will be true — there's an awful lot of **mis**information out there as well. If you come across something you are not sure of, or are confused or worried about, then ask someone you trust — preferably a parent, teacher, or some other adult you feel you can talk to.

But whatever you do, don't just bury your head in the sand and hope it will all go away. It won't. It's your life, take charge of it, enjoy it — and treat yourself and others with care.

2 EVERYBODY'S GOT SOME *kinda* BODY

THERE ARE TWO MAJOR THINGS TO KNOW ABOUT BODIES. ONE IS that they are always changing — the changes start the day we are born and continue right through our lives. (Just as well, really, otherwise we'd all be bald with big heads and pudgy arms and legs.) The other is that nobody's body is quite the same as anyone else's. So although the same kinds of changes happen to everybody, they happen in slightly different ways and at slightly different times.

▶ **THERE ARE TIMES** in our lives, though, when things change much more rapidly than at other times.

As babies we grow incredibly quickly. By the time a girl is one-and-a-half years old she will have reached nearly half her adult height. A boy reaches almost half his adult height at two years old.

Sometime between the ages of 10 and 14, we begin another growth spurt. And for the next few years our parents mutter about how we are "growing like beanstalks!"

Toward the end of the teenage years (around 18 for girls and 19 for boys), we reach our full adult height and whatever it is — little, lanky, or in-between — that's the height we are. But height isn't the only thing about us that changes.

CHECK IT OUT
Boys and girls grow at different rates. Girls grow more quickly than boys, but boys go on growing for longer.

I can't wait to be 17!

I'm glad I'm not 12!

I wish she still looked 17!

12 years

17 years

35 years

▶ **OUR BODY SHAPE** alters dramatically as we grow from children into adults—arms and legs get longer, hands and feet get bigger. Girls get wider hips and bigger breasts. Boys get broader chests and shoulders. Even the shape of our head and face changes.

Most of these changes happen when our sex organs start to develop (see next page). But other changes take place at different times in our lives, as well. Our weight can vary at any time, depending on what we eat and how much exercise we get. And, as we start to get old, our skin becomes wrinkled, our hair changes color, and we find it harder to move around.

▶ **EXACTLY WHEN** and how all these changes happen to us depends on a number of different things — whether we are male or female, for example, or what our parents look like, or the sort of food we eat, and how we live our lives.

The only thing we know for certain is that these changes will all happen, and (at some point) they'll happen to each and every one of us!

I wish he still looked 35!

70 years

THE LOVE OF YOUR LIFE!

Sometimes it's hard not to get hung up about the way we look. It's easy to think that the world is full of people who are better looking than us.

The weird thing is, just about everyone feels the same way about themselves. So, instead of worrying about it, try to be nice to your body and accept it for the way it is. And take good care of it — it's got to last you a lifetime!

My body is a temple.

▶ **WE ALL HAVE THE SAME** kinds of body parts. Everyone has a skeleton and muscles, a heart, lungs, stomach, and so on. The only parts that aren't the same for everyone are the sex organs. The sex organs are necessary for producing children, so they are also called the reproductive organs. They are what make men and women different.

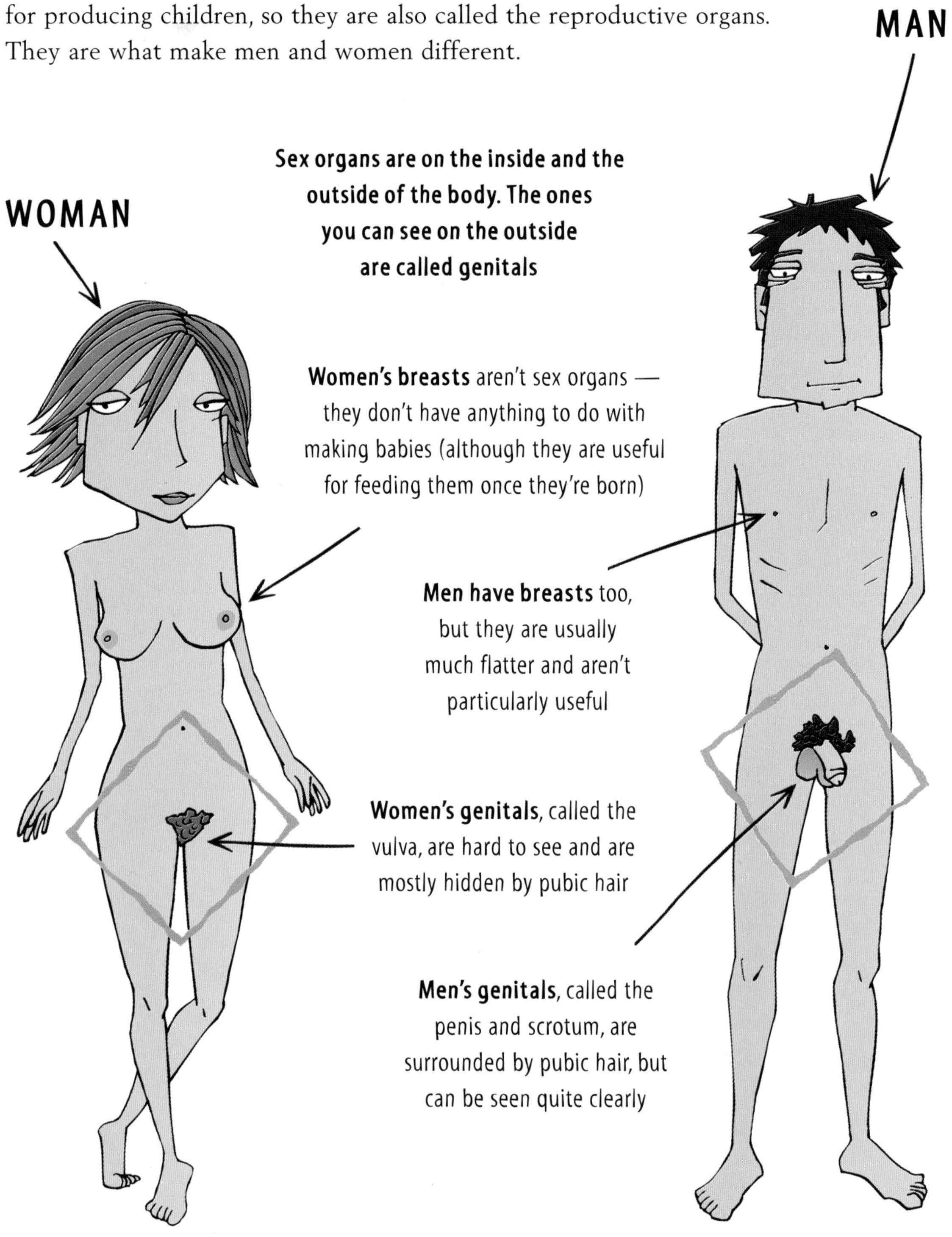

MAN

WOMAN

Sex organs are on the inside and the outside of the body. The ones you can see on the outside are called genitals

Women's breasts aren't sex organs — they don't have anything to do with making babies (although they are useful for feeding them once they're born)

Men have breasts too, but they are usually much flatter and aren't particularly useful

Women's genitals, called the vulva, are hard to see and are mostly hidden by pubic hair

Men's genitals, called the penis and scrotum, are surrounded by pubic hair, but can be seen quite clearly

THE TIME WHEN

our sex organs become fully developed is known as puberty. Like many scientific words, it comes from a Latin * word: *pubertas*, which means "grown-up."

And growing is what you do — up, out, and in all directions at once it sometimes feels like!

MOST OF THE CHANGES that

happen during puberty are physical ones — your body is changing from a child's body into an adult's body.

But this is one of those times when the body is way ahead of the mind, and the changes it puts you through also bring all sorts of new thoughts and emotions with them.

Sometimes, instead of puberty, people use the word "adolescence" (from

* **Latin** was the language spoken by the Ancient Romans. The Romans weren't only great at fighting and conquering people, they were pretty brainy as well.

puberti
pubertus

another Latin word). An adolescent is a young person who is neither a child nor an adult, but somewhere in-between.

It's a strange and often worrying time. In fact, it's a bit like being stuck on some kind of crazy roller coaster for a couple of years! Just remember that you will get through it. You will get used to your adult body, and all those seesawing emotions will settle down.

In the meantime, hold tight and try to enjoy it.

A C M E
PUBERTY
TIME BOMB

WHEN WILL I START?

Puberty can happen at any time from the age of 8 to 17, although most people begin between the ages of 10 and 14.

Remember, everybody's different. You might be the first in your class or the last and, although you might feel embarrassed to be so out of step, it is perfectly normal.

When you start puberty makes no difference to **how** you develop. No age is better than any other — there is simply the right age for you!

▶ **PUBERTY HAPPENS** because of special chemicals in your body called hormones. No, not Latin this time — it's from a Greek word: *hormon*, meaning "to set in motion." Which is pretty much what hormones do. They make things happen.

There are all sorts of hormones in your body. Each one does something different, but they all do it in the same sort of way. They travel around in your bloodstream turning different parts of you "on" or "off" — like switches.

CHECK IT OUT
The human body makes over 30 different types of hormones.

Plants have hormones too, you know!

Hormones tell your body when and where to start growing, and when to stop. They tell your stomach when to make digestive juices to break down food. They make your heart beat faster if you get angry or frightened, and send more energy to your muscles so that you can fight or run away.

They also tell your body when it's time for your sex organs to wake up and start doing their stuff. And that's when puberty hits you ...

The hormone story...

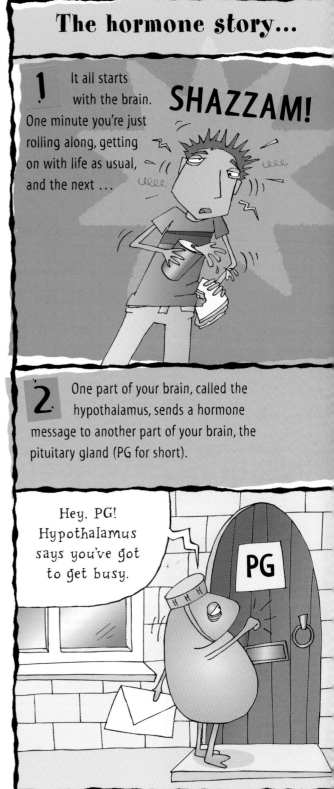

1 It all starts with the brain. One minute you're just rolling along, getting on with life as usual, and the next ...

SHAZZAM!

2 One part of your brain, called the hypothalamus, sends a hormone message to another part of your brain, the pituitary gland (PG for short).

Hey, PG! Hypothalamus says you've got to get busy.

PG

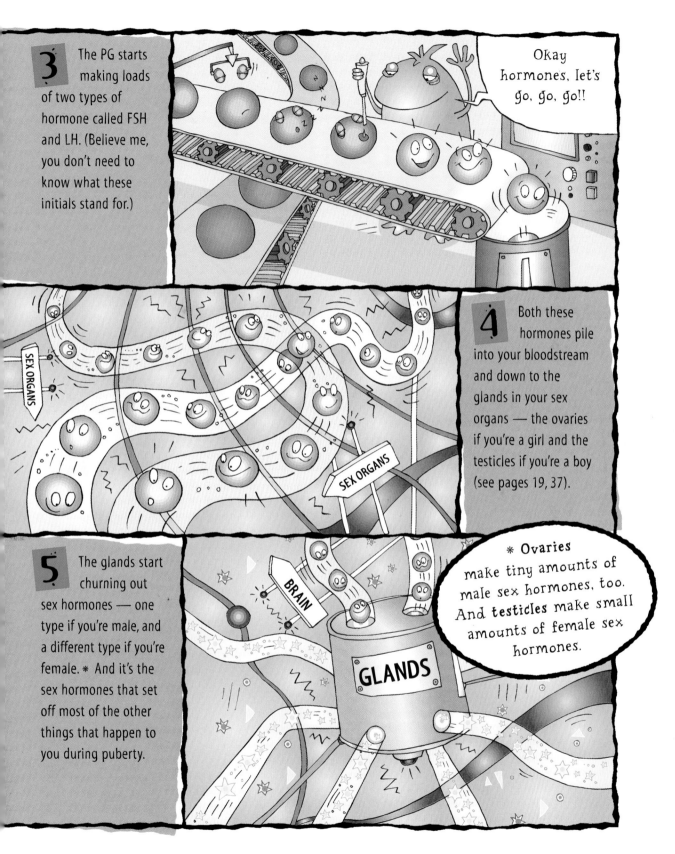

3 The PG starts making loads of two types of hormone called FSH and LH. (Believe me, you don't need to know what these initials stand for.)

Okay hormones, let's go, go, go!!

4 Both these hormones pile into your bloodstream and down to the glands in your sex organs — the ovaries if you're a girl and the testicles if you're a boy (see pages 19, 37).

SEX ORGANS

SEX ORGANS

5 The glands start churning out sex hormones — one type if you're male, and a different type if you're female. * And it's the sex hormones that set off most of the other things that happen to you during puberty.

BRAIN

GLANDS

* **Ovaries** make tiny amounts of male sex hormones, too. And **testicles** make small amounts of female sex hormones.

BOYS USUALLY START PUBERTY SOMEWHERE BETWEEN THE AGES OF 11 and 14. This is often a bit later than girls, which may explain why some of the girls you know could suddenly seem to be towering over you. Don't worry, you'll soon catch up!

PUBERTY ALERT

Wow, what a list! Don't panic, not all of these happen at the same time.

▷ Arms and legs get longer
▷ Hands and feet get larger
▷ Height and weight increase
▷ Face lengthens — nose and jaw become bigger
▷ Body sweats more
▷ Facial hair grows
▷ Hair on arms, legs, and chest can grow darker and thicker
▷ Hair grows under the arms
▷ Voice "breaks" and becomes deeper; Adam's apple in throat gets larger
▷ Shoulders and chest get bigger
▷ Pubic hair grows around genitals
▷ Penis gets larger and longer
▷ Scrotum gets bigger and baggier and turns a darker color
▷ Testicles get larger and fuller
▷ Testicles produce sperm
▷ Penis ejaculates sperm, sometimes during "wet dreams"
▷ Hair and skin can become oily and skin may break out

▶ **AT FIRST, ALL** the changes happen on the inside of your body, when your testicles start producing male sex hormones. One of the main male sex hormones is testosterone. This is the one that switches on the sperm-making factory in your testicles.

> I'm a sperm machine!

As far as your body is concerned, making sperm is really what life is all about. Sperm is one-half of what it takes to make a baby, and as soon as your body starts producing it you can become a dad — now that is scary!

Testicles are the two round things inside your scrotum. They start off small to begin with, about the size of marbles, and they don't do doing anything but hang there. But during puberty they grow to the size of walnuts or small plums.

An adult male testicle is about 1½ in. (4 cm) long and about 1 in. (3 cm) wide, and weighs about as much as two Brazil nuts.

Inside and out...

Get to know your sex organs on the inside as well as the outside.
It's up to you to take care of them and keep them in good working order.

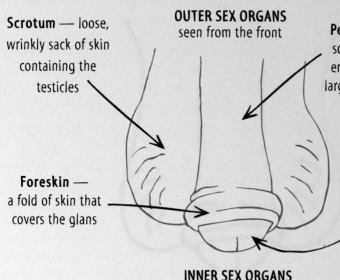

OUTER SEX ORGANS
seen from the front

Scrotum — loose, wrinkly sack of skin containing the testicles

Penis — usually soft and squishy except during an erection. Then it becomes larger and harder and sticks out from the body

Glans — the tip of the penis. Contains a small opening through which urine and sperm leave the body, but never at the same time

Foreskin — a fold of skin that covers the glans

INNER SEX ORGANS
seen from the front

Vas deferens — tubes that carry sperm from the epididymis to the urethra

Bladder — not a sex organ but connected to them. It stores urine, which is liquid waste from the body

Seminal vesicles — these and the prostate gland produce fluids that keep sperm healthy and help them flow along. The sperm mix with the fluids to make a milky liquid called semen

Epididymis — thin, scrunched-up tubes that store newly-made sperm for about four or five weeks

Prostate gland — see "seminal vesicles"

Testicles — produce sperm and the hormone testosterone

Urethra — tube that carries urine from the bladder, and semen from the seminal vesicles and the vas deferens

Be smart, wear a plastic sports protector or "cup" to protect your testicles when you're playing contact sports, and never kick another boy there — unless you want to make an enemy for life!

▶ **AS THE TESTICLES** grow, the scrotum gets a bit baggier and saggier. The skin may go darker than the rest of you, and even a bit pimply. Often, one testicle hangs a bit lower than the other — usually the left one. This helps to protect them from banging against each other when you're jumping around.

The reason that testicles hang outside the body has to do with body heat. Sperm can only be made in a temperature that's a couple of degrees lower than your normal body temperature. (Which is why your testicles shrivel up and cling to you in the cold, and get all loose and dangly when it's hot.)

Although this is great for your sperm, it's not as good for you. Testicles are easily hurt and it's important to take care of them. If they get hit or kicked the pain is often excruciating, and they could be permanently damaged.

▶ **ONCE YOU START** producing sperm, the sperm start traveling. Sperm have to grow up, too, and while they're doing it they leave the testicles and gradually work their way along an incredibly long, thin tube called the epididymis.

Um ... you're sure this is the right way?

Each testicle has its own epididymis coiled around one half of it like cotton wrapped around an egg. (If you could unwind an epididymis it would be about 6 1/2 yards/6 meters long.)

It takes about two weeks for a sperm to mature. Then it hangs around in the epididymis until it is either ejaculated (leaves the body through the penis), or is absorbed back into the body.

My gonads are goners!

EJACULATION HAPPENS when muscles at the base of your penis contract, or squeeze together. This sends sperm shooting out of the epididymis into a shorter, thicker tube called the vas deferens.

OTHER WORDS FOR
Penis — dick, prick, cock, wang, pecker ... to name but a few.

As the sperm race along the vas deferens they mix with fluids from two glands (the seminal vesicles and the prostate gland). This sticky, whitish mixture of sperm and other stuff is called semen.

Finally, the semen arrives at the urethra. This tube leads down through the penis to an opening at the tip. This small opening is where your urine comes out when you pee, and it's where semen comes out when you ejaculate. (And, no, it's not physically possible to do both at the same time.)

Who needs billions, when one will do?

In most cases, though, before you can ejaculate (or "come"), you need to have an erection — this is when your penis gets thicker and stiffer and sticks out from your body.

Supersperm!

◆ Once you've started making sperm, you usually go on producing it for the rest of your life.

◆ Sperm are tiny — a single sperm is less than half a millimeter long.

◆ On average, an adult male makes around 200 MILLION sperm every day. Over 60-odd years that's about 4,500 BILLION sperm!

◆ Before it leaves the body, sperm mixes with other fluids to make a milky liquid called semen.

◆ An average ejaculation contains about a teaspoonful of semen. One teaspoonful of semen may contain about 400 million sperm.

◆ It takes just ONE sperm to make a baby.

◆ Sperm that isn't ejaculated dissolves and is absorbed back into the body.

Seen under a microscope, a sperm looks a bit like a tadpole with an incredibly skinny, whip-like tail that's about ten times as long as its head.

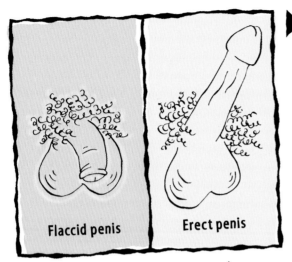

Flaccid penis | **Erect penis**

A **flaccid (soft) penis** hangs downward.
An erect penis gets thicker and longer and sticks up and out from the body.

▶ **YOU GET AN** erection when blood rushes into your penis and fills up all the tiny spaces inside it. (Like water filling up a spongy balloon.) Muscles around your penis tighten to hold in all this extra blood so that your penis stays stiff. When the muscles relax, the blood flows away and your penis goes soft again.

You can have erections before you reach puberty. Even very young boys sometimes feel their penis getting stiff. But although this might give you some nice tickly feelings in the pit of your stomach, nothing else happens and your penis soon goes back to normal.

OTHER WORDS FOR
Erection — hard-on, boner, woody

▶ **DURING PUBERTY,** though, things change. As far as the body is concerned, the purpose of an erection is to make it possible for a man to have sexual intercourse (see page 72). So men usually get an erection when they're feeling sexually excited, or "horny."

But in fact, it's not quite as straight-forward as that — because men have erections for other reasons, too. They can have them when they are feeling warm and relaxed, when they see someone attractive, or when they are just having happy thoughts and sex is the last thing on their mind.

Oh no, this is my stop! Go down, go down!

To begin with, you'll probably find yourself having erections at the strangest times and in the weirdest places — on buses, in the shower, even in the middle of a math lesson.

It might seem like your penis has taken on a life of its own. You can't control it and it's easy to feel embarrassed by it. Don't be! It's all perfectly normal. It's just your body getting used to some of those new sensations that puberty brings.

What do girls think about penises?

Mostly they don't think about them at all. Girls are much more interested in how boys behave.

> He's SO boring ... always boasting about having a big you-know-what!

PENIS PERILS — No. 1:
SIZE

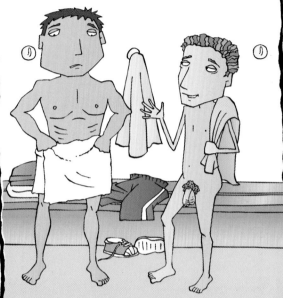

Most boys worry about the size of their penis, particularly during puberty — probably because they all think that bigger must be better. It isn't.

The size of your penis has nothing to do with how manly you are, or how good a lover you will be, or how much money you have! In fact, as long as everything is working properly, size makes no difference at all — at least, not to anyone other than a teenage boy.

It's far more important to be interested in other people than in the size of your penis — whatever it is. And, anyway, penises are forever changing their size and shape. Whenever you're cold or nervous yours will shrink, and when you have an erection it'll get bigger. In fact, as it turns out, most erect adult penises are all pretty much the same size.

PENIS PERILS — No. 2: BENDY ONES

Lots of penises bend at an angle when they're erect. They may curve upward, or off to one side. It's nothing to worry about. Bendy penises are as normal as the color of your hair or the size of your feet. As long as everything else is in good working order, a bendy penis is no different than a non-bendy one.

▶ **YOU DON'T ALWAYS** come when you have an erection. If you do your best to ignore it and think about something else, it will usually just fade away.

Occasionally — especially in the beginning — you might find yourself leaking a drop or two of semen with even the smallest erection.

If this happens when you're out and about, the best thing to do is to go to the bathroom and clean yourself up with a tissue. And make sure you change your underwear every day — dried semen can get a bit smelly!

▶ **YOU CAN GIVE** yourself an erection and make yourself come by touching or rubbing your penis. This is known as masturbating.

Some people think masturbation is wrong, but it's a perfectly natural thing to do, and almost everyone does it at some time or another.

Masturbating makes your body feel very hot and tingly and excited. These feelings get stronger and stronger until you ejaculate, and then they fade away. Sometimes the feelings are so powerful a huge wave of pleasure crashes over you. This is called having an orgasm.

Girls masturbate and have orgasms, too, but they do it in a slightly different way (see page 46). Also, men and women have orgasms when they have sexual intercourse. (Although not every time, and often not at the same time!)

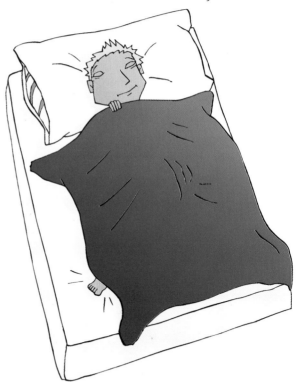

OTHER WORDS FOR
Masturbating — jerking off, beating off, whacking off (usually applies to male masturbation only)

OTHER WORDS FOR

Semen — come (sometimes spelled "cum"), spunk, jism

▶**FOR MANY BOYS,** the first time they ejaculate might be a complete surprise. They might not even realize that they're doing it. At least, not until they wake up in the morning and find a dollop of wet, sticky, or dried semen on their bedsheets.

Ejaculating in your sleep is known as having a "wet dream."

You might remember having an exciting or sexy dream, or it might all be a total mystery. You might have just a few wet dreams, or a lot. You might get your first wet dream early on in puberty or quite late. Or, you might not have any wet dreams at all.

However it happens, it's okay! You haven't wet the bed, you're not ill, and it's not your fault. It's just your body, getting itself organized and making sure that everything's working properly. Don't panic, and don't hide the laundry from your mom, or dad, or whoever does it. They'll understand.

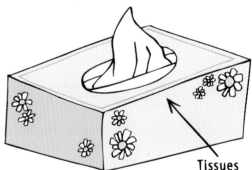

Tissues

PENIS PERILS — No. 3:
BUMPY ONES

Lumps and bumps are a bit trickier than bends. Your penis is covered in skin and, like the skin on the rest of your body, it can develop pimples or moles. These are usually nothing to worry about. Small, whitish spots or pimples around your penis or testicles can be caused by your sweat glands kicking into gear, or the growth of your pubic hair.

But lumps and bumps on your penis or testicles could be anything, from plain old warts to something more serious, so don't be foolish and ignore it — GO AND SEE A DOCTOR.

Oh no! I think it's getting smaller!

▶ **AS A PENIS** grows, its foreskin grows too. The foreskin is a close-fitting, double layer of skin that folds down over the head of the penis like a hood.

The head of the penis is called the glans. It's shaped a bit like the cap of a mushroom and it's the most sensitive part of the penis. The foreskin protects

▶ **YOUR PENIS GROWS** in size during puberty, just like the rest of you. But don't kid yourself — this can be a slow process and you might not notice much change (if any) for at least a year or so after your testicles get bigger.

This can feel like a disaster if all your friends seem to be well ahead of you. But everyone gets there in the end, and early or late it makes no difference.

Remember too, that lots of boys fall into the trap of boasting about the size of their penises — and much of that is wishful thinking!

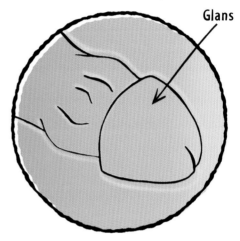

Glans

When the foreskin is pulled back, the glans (head of the penis) is fully exposed.

PENIS PERILS — No. 4: CIRCUMCISION

This is an operation in which part or all of the foreskin is cut away from the penis. Many Jewish and Muslim people do this for religious reasons — usually soon after birth. But other families do it too — some for religious or traditional reasons; some because they think it is fashionable.

People used to believe that it was healthier and cleaner to have a circumcised penis, but these days we know that there is really no medical proof of that, and some men who have been circumcised think that it makes the head of the penis less sensitive.

Very occasionally, circumcision might be necessary if an older boy or man finds that his foreskin is too tight to slide comfortably back and forth . However, there can be other solutions for that, too, so if you have any problems with your foreskin, talk to a doctor!

From the side...

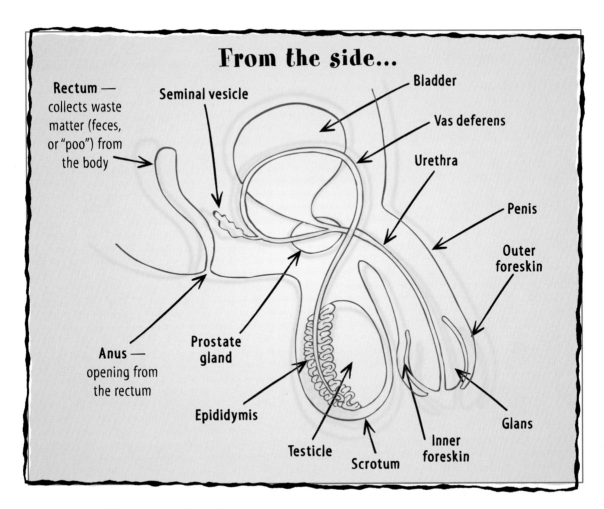

Rectum — collects waste matter (feces, or "poo") from the body

Seminal vesicle

Bladder

Vas deferens

Urethra

Penis

Outer foreskin

Anus — opening from the rectum

Prostate gland

Epididymis

Testicle

Scrotum

Inner foreskin

Glans

the glans and keeps it soft and moist.

The foreskins of babies and young boys often completely cover their glans, leaving just a small hole at the tip to urinate through. At first, the inner layer of the foreskin is tightly attached to the glans and can't easily be pulled back. (It's also not a good idea to try, as it could separate the foreskin too soon.)

At some point during childhood, the foreskin loosens naturally so that it can slide backward and forward over the glans. The reason you have a foreskin is to allow plenty of room for the skin to unfold along the penis when it is erect.

▶ **ONCE THE FORESKIN** has separated, its inner layer produces small amounts of whitish, creamy stuff called smegma (from a Greek word that means soap). Smegma keeps the glans and foreskin soft and oiled and working smoothly, but it can get very smelly if it is left to build up under the foreskin.

Keep your glans and foreskin clean by gently sliding the foreskin back and washing all round it with soapy water once a day. Use a nonperfumed soap and make sure you rinse all the soap off and dry well afterward.

How to survive a close shave...

Shaving can be a tricky business; it's all too easy to give yourself scrapes, cuts, and sore skin! Electric shavers are easy to use, but can act like sandpaper on soft skin. Razors are gentler on the skin, but need to be handled slowly and smoothly ...

Start by washing your face in warm water. Warm water opens up the hair follicles in your skin, which means the blade tugs less on the hairs.

Then spread shaving cream around and under your chin and over your top lip. Plain soap works fine, too.

Work from below the ear on each side and toward the center. Don't press on the razor too hard. Use small strokes and rinse the blade in warm water after each stroke.

Follow the way the hair grows. Shaving against the hair can give you a rash.

Rinse with cold water to close up the follicles again, then pat your face dry.

Aftershave lotion closes up the follicles, too, but it can sting and make your skin very dry and flaky. Use a face moisturizer when you've finished.

▶ **SO, WHAT ELSE** grows during puberty? Well, you get a lot hairier, for one thing. Hair on your arms and legs grows darker and coarser, and sometimes on your chest, stomach, and belly, too.

Pubic hair grows around your penis and testicles and, later on, hair grows in your armpits as well.

And, at some point, the hairs around your mouth and chin start to grow.

Facial hair usually shows up on your top lip first, then spreads to your cheeks and chin. It's soft to start with, but grows thicker and coarser as time goes on.

At some point, you'll want to start shaving, but don't rush to shave before you really need to. Just think, once you do start you'll be doing it every day (or so) for the rest of your life — unless you like wearing a carpet on your face!

▶ **PUBERTY IS** a real sweat. On top of everything else, all those hormones rampaging around your body make your sweat glands go into overtime.

Sweat glands lie just underneath the top layer of your skin. You've got millions of them all over your body — but especially in your armpits, around your genitals, and on the soles of your feet.

Sweating helps to cool the body down, but you don't only sweat when you're hot. You sweat when you're nervous or excited, and sometimes when you're not doing anything at all.

Dried sweat is a good place for bacteria to be and that's when sweat starts to smell. Everyone sweats, and we all get a bit smelly from time to time, but there's a very simple solution — wash your body, from head to toe, every day.

▶ **AND THEN THERE** are the dreaded pimples! Just when you think you've got everything under control, your skin breaks out in enormous lumps and bumps and your face turns into a pizza.

Along with the sweat glands in your skin there are oil glands, too. The oil, called sebum, helps protect your skin and hair and keep it waterproof and supple. But you can have too much of a good thing — especially during puberty.

Every hair on your body has its own oil gland alongside it, and when too much sebum builds up it can block the follicle — the tiny tube in which the hair grows.

When sebum collects on the surface

of the follicle it makes a blackhead. If it forms below the skin it makes a whitehead, usually with a red lump. Too much sebum also makes your hair very greasy and this can give you pimples around your hairline and forehead.

Washing your hair every few days

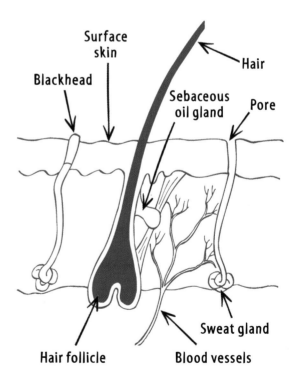

A **close-up look** at a slice of skin shows millions of tiny pores, or holes, as well as hair follicles.

and keeping your skin clean will help. Use a mild soap, or if your skin is dry use a soapless face wash. (Too much soap can irritate the skin; dry skin cracks, letting bacteria in.) Use an oil-free moisturizing cream, too, and keep your hands and especially your fingernails clean and away from your face.

If you have lots of pimples on your face, neck, or back, then you may have acne. In this case, go and see your doctor. If it is acne, there are a number of different treatments you can try that your doctor will be able to tell you about.

Keeping it clean!

⊙ Take a bath or shower every day if possible. If not, make sure you wash your armpits, genitals, and feet.

⊙⊙ Wear clean socks and underwear every day. Natural materials like cotton are less likely to trap odors than synthetics.

PHEW!

⊙⊙⊙ Deodorants and antiperspirants can help, but don't go wild with them, or use them instead of washing. Don't use them around your genitals, either, as they could give you a rash. Choose whichever type works best for you. Deodorants work on the smell. Antiperspirants make you sweat less by blocking the pores (tiny sweat holes) in your skin — if this gives you a rash, look for an alcohol-free brand or just stick with soap or a body wash.

TALKING ABOUT doctors ... you'll find more stuff on health problems in chapter 8, but if you are worried about your body or your health in any way, books are not the answer. You need to see a doctor.

Lots of boys find it difficult to talk to a doctor about anything personal — particularly if it's about their penis! It will help if you can talk the problem over first with your mom or dad, or another adult you feel you can trust — if only to get them to make an appointment for you with the family doctor. But if you really can't do this, then you'll have to take a deep breath and make an appointment for yourself.

Most family doctors belong to a group practice. This means there are a number of different doctors in the practice, both male and female, and you can ask to see a male doctor. But, if that isn't possible, just remember that doctors really have seen it all before — whether they're young or old, male or female — and they will keep anything you tell them private, even if they do know your parents.

And after all, what is worse — a few minutes of embarrassment, or weeks spent worrying about whether or not your penis is going to drop off?

Well ... er ... uhm ... er ...

4 | GIRL STUFF

FOR MANY GIRLS, PUBERTY STARTS UP SOMEWHERE BETWEEN THE AGES of 10 and 13, but it can start much earlier — as young as eight — or much later — not until 16 or 17. Some girls get there at around the same age as their mothers, so you could try asking your mom, but don't be too worried if this isn't the case. There's no particular rhyme or reason to the time puberty starts. It's all up to your body's internal clock.

▶ **AS SOON AS** sex hormones start zipping around inside you, your body will begin to change. It's not as if you suddenly turn into some sort of female werewolf (although there might be times when you feel like you have!). A lot of the changes happen quite slowly, and you may not even be aware of them for a while.

You might notice your shape changing first. Most girls put on weight and their hips and waist get curvier during puberty. How curvy you get, of course, depends on your natural body shape, and everyone's is different.

All of a sudden, you become very aware of your body, and how it looks — or at least how you think it looks. You also start noticing other girls' shapes — and comparing them with your own.

I don't have any curves.

I've got lots!

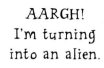

AARGH! I'm turning into an alien.

WE'RE SURROUNDED by photos of models and pop stars. They all look very glamorous — with perfect skin, hair, teeth, and figures.

It's all too easy to start thinking that if our body doesn't look like theirs, then there must be something wrong with it.

The thing is, fashion models and pop stars are paid to look glamorous. It's their job, and most of them spend a huge amount of time, effort, and money making themselves look that way.

It might seem as if they don't have a care in the world, but they are always worrying about whether their face and figure are still in fashion.

MOST WOMEN don't look like stars, they look like themselves — lumps, bumps, bad hair, and all.

Everyone has parts of their body that they like more than others. The trick is to try to accept ALL your parts and be happy with who you are. That way, you'll spend less time worrying about how you look, and more on being interested in the people and things going on around you.

ON PLANET PUBERTY
Here's what to expect, but don't worry — it won't all happen at once!

- ○ Height and weight increases
- ○ Face widens and lengthens a little
- ○ Hips get wider and more curvy
- ○ Arms and legs get longer
- ○ Hands and feet get larger
- ○ Voice deepens a little
- ○ Pubic hair grows
- ○ Hair on arms and legs grows darker and more visible
- ○ Hair grows under the arms
- ○ Breasts and nipples get larger
- ○ Nipples may darken in color
- ○ Internal and external sex organs become larger and more developed
- ○ Vagina produces a sticky, whitish liquid
- ○ Ovaries begin releasing eggs
- ○ Periods start
- ○ Hair and skin become oily and pimply
- ○ Body sweats more

▶ **ONE CHANGE YOU** will notice is when your nipples and breasts start to swell. Your nipples will feel harder and more sensitive, the circle of skin around them (the areola) might get darker, and your breasts will ache a bit sometimes.

Breasts grow slowly and not always at the same time. Sometimes one side will be bigger than the other. That's OK! It doesn't mean you will be lopsided forever. They will even out in the end, although few breasts are ever exactly equal.

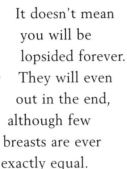

▶ **SOME GIRLS ARE** thrilled when their breasts start to form and they can't wait to wear a bra. It makes them feel feminine and more grown up. But not everyone feels that way, and unless your breasts are quite large and heavy you don't have to wear a bra if you don't want to. (Although you might need to wear one for sports.)

When you do decide to buy a bra, it's a good idea to get yourself measured first. Go to the lingerie department in a large store, or to a speciality store, and ask one of the assistants to measure you. (Take your mom, big sister, or a friend if you feel nervous.) Many stores offer this as a free service,

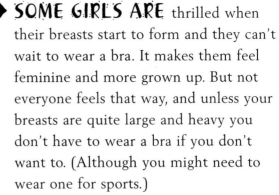

I can't find mine?

BREAST BEATING

The reason you have breasts is to make milk to feed your baby (if you have one), and the size of them has no effect on how much milk they will make. Their size and shape come from the protective fat that forms around the glands that make the milk.

Girls often worry about the size and shape of their breasts. It's easy to do, when magazines and movies make such a fuss about them.

Most men think breasts are attractive and sexy, and most boys soon learn to think the same way. But in spite of what YOU might think, there isn't any one perfect shape or size. Like everything else to do with the body, breasts come in all shapes and sizes, and they are all equally perfect in their own way.

OOCH! OUCH!

HAIRY SCARY

Shaving is quick and easy for legs and armpits, but BE WARNED, it strengthens the hairs and they grow back even coarser. DON'T shave your face or stomach.

Single hairs can be plucked out with tweezers, or cut if the hair grows from a mole. Or you can use chemicals to bleach hair or to remove it, but you need to be careful with these, as the wrong type can harm or even scar your skin.

There's also waxing — using strips of soft wax to pull the hairs out. This weakens the hair growth over time and it lasts longer than shaving. But it's expensive, and a bit painful — think of ripping off bandages!

and their assistants are trained to measure and give advice on bra sizes.

You will be measured in a changing room and will probably be asked to take your top off so you can be measured bare-chested. Don't worry if you feel embarrassed, everybody does.

▶ **ANOTHER CHANGE** that's hard to miss is when you get hairier. The hairs on your arms and legs get darker, and pubic hair starts appearing around your external sex organs (see page 45). You might also see a line of darker hair running down from your navel (belly button) to your pubic hair.

The hairs on your top lip might get a bit darker, too. Hair will grow in your armpits, and you might have a few dark hairs around your nipples.

In many parts of the world it's fashionable to pretend that the only place women have any hair is on their heads! (Even men are starting to feel self-conscious about too much body hair.)

But fashions come and go, and having hair on your body is perfectly normal. If it doesn't bother you, leave it where it is. If you want to remove some of it, think carefully about how you are going to do it. Get some advice first. Ask your mom or another older woman what she does.

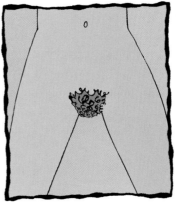

Pubic hair mostly grows in a triangle that covers your vagina. But you may have a few dark hairs on your tummy and the tops of your legs, too.

▶ **AND WHILE ALL** this is happening on the outside, on the inside your ovaries are churning out female sex hormones.

It's the female sex hormones (mainly estrogen and progesterone) that are responsible for most of the changes that happen to your body. They make your sex organs grow bigger, too (although you don't really notice because they're mostly on the inside). And when your sex organs have grown enough, more hormones from your brain tell your ovaries to start sending out their eggs.

▶ **OVARIES CONTAIN** hundreds of thousands of tiny eggs, called ova (a single egg is an ovum). An ovum is one half of what it takes to make a baby. The other half is a male sperm (see pages 18–21). Put the two together and — BINGO! A baby starts growing!

Every girl is born with all her eggs

EGGS-TRAORDINARY!

-))) A single human egg is about half the size of this period ———→ .
-))) Your ovaries store hundreds of thousands of eggs, but only about 600 of them will ever mature.
-))) Eggs stop maturing and periods stop happening in your late 40s or early 50s. This is called menopause.

already inside her. At first the eggs are only half formed, but once puberty begins the eggs start to mature (grow up) — usually just one egg at a time.

When an egg is ready, it pushes its way out of its ovary and into the nearest fallopian tube. The egg then travels along the fallopian tube until it reaches the uterus or womb.

▶ **AT THE SAME TIME,** the womb is getting ready for its arrival. A thick lining grows on the inside wall of the womb, like an extra-thick blanket stuffed with tiny blood vessels. The lining is there to protect and feed the egg while it is growing, but the egg will ONLY grow if it has been fertilized * by a sperm first.

If the egg hasn't been fertilized, it breaks up and dissolves. Then the lining breaks up as well. Mixed with some blood, the lining oozes out of the womb into the vagina, and then out of the vaginal opening. This leaking of blood

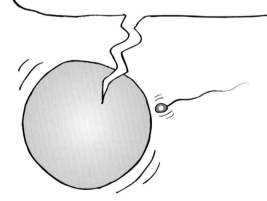

* **A fertilized egg** is one that has joined up with a male sperm — see pages 74-75. The sperm has to push its head right into the center of the egg. Usually, only one sperm can fertilize one egg at a time.

The inside story...

You may not be able to see your internal sex organs, but it's a good idea to know where they are, and what they do.

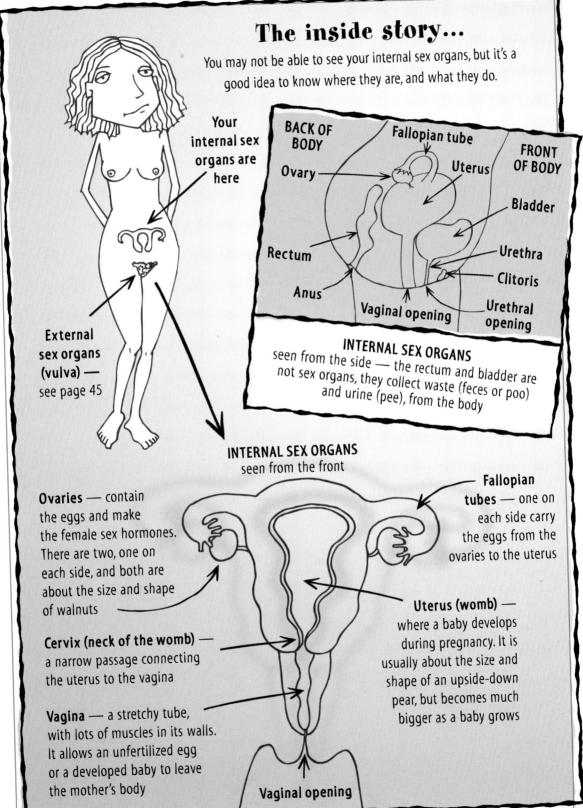

Your internal sex organs are here

External sex organs (vulva) — see page 45

BACK OF BODY

FRONT OF BODY

Ovary

Fallopian tube

Uterus

Bladder

Urethra

Clitoris

Rectum

Anus

Vaginal opening

Urethral opening

INTERNAL SEX ORGANS
seen from the side — the rectum and bladder are not sex organs, they collect waste (feces or poo) and urine (pee), from the body

INTERNAL SEX ORGANS
seen from the front

Ovaries — contain the eggs and make the female sex hormones. There are two, one on each side, and both are about the size and shape of walnuts

Cervix (neck of the womb) — a narrow passage connecting the uterus to the vagina

Vagina — a stretchy tube, with lots of muscles in its walls. It allows an unfertilized egg or a developed baby to leave the mother's body

Fallopian tubes — one on each side carry the eggs from the ovaries to the uterus

Uterus (womb) — where a baby develops during pregnancy. It is usually about the size and shape of an upside-down pear, but becomes much bigger as a baby grows

Vaginal opening

The uterus is about 7.5 cm long and 5 cm wide at the top. It's hollow inside and its muscly walls are almost 2.5 cm thick.

and bits of clotty stuff from the vagina is called having a period, and it happens roughly every 28 days.

▶ **HAVING YOUR FIRST** period is the most dramatic sign of puberty for a girl, and it's a big event. It's exciting to know that your body is doing what it should — but it can also be scary suddenly to find blood in your panties.

Lots of girls feel embarrassed at the thought of having periods, and nervous about how they will cope with them. Many wish they didn't have them at all — who wants all that mess and hassle! And as soon as you start having periods, it means you can get pregnant and have babies — HELP!

Relax! Having periods is a nuisance sometimes, but it's all part of being female, and of who you are. You soon get used to dealing with them — and just because your body has started growing up, it doesn't mean you have to turn

Guess what! My periods have started.

Lucky you, wish mine would.

Hope mine never start!

Next period due ... NOW!

COUNT DOWN

It's a good idea to keep a record of when your periods are due, mainly so you can be sure to have sanitary pads or tampons on hand (see page 41). But the timing of your period will vary a little from month to month, especially at first.

Generally, your next period starts about 28 days from the first day of your previous one. So the first day of your period counts as Day 1, and your next period will start on Day 29 — which then becomes Day 1 again.

But everyone is different, of course, so some women have periods every 21 days, and some every 35. And some never really settle into a regular cycle at all.

into an adult overnight. You're still the same person you were before, and you've still got plenty of time to do the rest of your growing up.

▶ **A PERIOD CAN** last for anything from three to eight days — although mostly they take about five.

How much you bleed varies from person to person and even from month to month. Sometimes a period will be quite light — not much more than a few brownish smears — and other times it will be heavier. Some girls always have heavy flows, and others light.

For the first year or so you may find that your periods don't follow any particular pattern or monthly cycle. In fact, some girls never settle into a regular cycle at all. And even if you are fairly regular, there may still be times when you miss a period. Illness, stress, or even

travel can all affect your monthly cycle.

It's quite common, at first, to have one period and then nothing for a few months, or even to have two periods in the same month. So don't worry if your periods are irregular when they start.

However, periods also stop when you are pregnant, so if you have had sex with someone then it is possible that you could be pregnant (see chapter 7). If you are at all worried about anything to do with your periods, talk to your mom, a doctor, or the school nurse.

OTHER WORDS FOR
Periods — menstruation, monthly, the curse, or being on the rag

► **THE BAD NEWS** is that, at some time or another, most girls get cramps when they have a period. Cramps are an aching pain low down in your belly. They usually happen at the start of a period, or a day or two before. They last for a day or so, and vary from mild to agony!

Periods can also make your breasts feel sore, and your body heavy and bloated. And you can feel washed out, grumpy, sad, and deeply miserable. The worst thing is, one minute you want to hide in a corner and sob, and the next you want to kick someone — and you don't even know why!

► **THIS IS THE DEMON** PMS, or premenstrual syndrome (also known as PMT, premenstrual tension). Like cramps, PMS can turn up a day or two before your period begins, so you don't always realize what's causing your evil mood. Not every girl gets it, especially at first, but it can build up over time.

I think I'm going to die!

PERIOD PANIC — No 1:
PAINFUL PERIODS

If the pain isn't too bad — more of a grumble than a howl — try walking or some other type of light exercise. It may sound like the last thing you want to do, but it really can help (honest!). But if the pains gets very strong, it's best to take a painkiller and lie down with a heating pad on your belly to help you relax. Or you could try relaxing in a hot bath.

Some girls hardly have cramps at all, or only very mildly. But a few poor souls get them badly almost every month. If you are one of the unlucky ones, DON'T suffer in silence. Go and see your doctor; there are a number of things he or she can do to help. If you find it difficult to talk about it, take someone with you, such as your mom, or another adult you can talk to.

WHEN YOU DON'T have cramps or PMS, though, there's no reason why your life shouldn't go on as normal. Having a period doesn't mean that you can't go out, go dancing, climb trees, or do any of the things you normally do. You just have to make sure that you are wearing the right kind of protection.

This means wearing some kind of sanitary pad or tampon to soak up the blood from your vagina.

SANITARY PADS are strips of padded material that fit inside your underpants. You buy them in different sizes and thicknesses, depending on how heavy or light your period is.

Most have a strip of sticky tape on one side to hold the pad in place on your panties. Some also have side flaps called wings. These are sticky-backed too and fold under the crotch of your panties for extra grip.

Pads are easy and quick to use, especially when you are getting used to your periods. But they are a bit bulky to carry and you can't wear them when you go swimming.

PERIOD PANIC — No 2: PMS

If you find yourself getting a lot more emotional than usual just before your period, try to remember that it could be PMS. Think twice before you decide to chop up all your clothes or snap at someone.

There's no magical cure for PMS, and not very much you can do about it. You just have to wait for it to blow over. Try to make your life a little less stressful. You might find it's best just to stay at home and be by yourself for a while. Or maybe hide out with a good friend. Taking vitamin B6, evening primrose oil, calcium, or magnesium supplements can help — or see your doctor.

CHECK IT OUT

Before sanitary pads were invented, women tore up pieces of soft cloth into strips. They folded the strips into squares and tucked them inside their underwear. If you get caught without a pad or a tampon, fold a long strip of toilet paper into a pad and tuck it inside your panties to soak up the blood. Or you could use paper tissues, cotton hankies, or even a cotton sock!

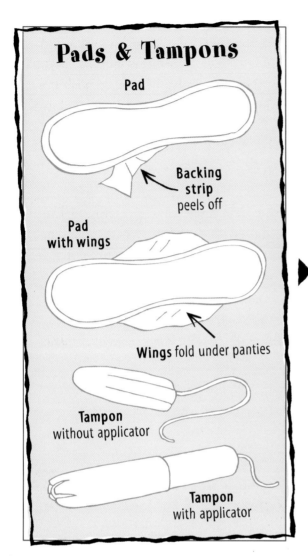

Pads & Tampons

Pad

Backing strip peels off

Pad with wings

Wings fold under panties

Tampon without applicator

Tampon with applicator

be pulled out again to change it.

Like pads, tampons are sold in different thicknesses. Some have just a tear-off plastic wrapping and are pushed into the vagina with your fingers. Others come inside a cardboard or plastic applicator. By sliding the bottom half of the applicator upward, it pushes the tampon out and into your vagina. You then throw the applicator away.

▶ **THE GOOD THING** about tampons is that they are completely invisible to wear (except for the string), and they can be worn with any kind of tight-fitting clothes or a swimsuit.

The downside is that, to begin with anyway, they are a bit tricky to use, and many girls find the thought of pushing something into their vagina a bit creepy.

However, you don't have to wear a tampon if you don't want to. And, in any case, it's quite a good idea to start off using pads — just having periods is enough to cope with, at first.

▶ **TAMPONS ARE JUST** about the same size as your thumb, and they have a piece of string attached to one end of them. They are made of the same material as pads, but it's compressed (squeezed) tightly together.

Tampons are pushed up inside the vagina. Once there, they swell up to fit snugly to the vaginal walls and soak up the blood before it comes out of the vaginal opening. The piece of string is left hanging out of the vagina so that the tampon can

▶ **AT SOME POINT,** though, you might find yourself wondering what tampons feel like. If so, take a chance and try one out — just for fun.

Tampon boxes have a pamphlet inside that explains how to use them. Or you could try asking a friend or your mom. Use the smallest size, and try to relax as much as you can so that your vaginal muscles aren't tensed up. Take a few deep breaths.

Make sure that you know where your vaginal opening is (see the diagram on page 45) and that the tampon and your hands are clean. It's important that you don't get any germs inside your vagina, otherwise you could get ill.

You have to push the whole tampon right up inside the vagina. You shouldn't be able to feel it once it is in place. If you can, then you probably need to push it a bit higher. Leave the string hanging down.

▶ **YOU SHOULD CHANGE** your pad or tampon regularly — at least every three or four hours during the day, as well as last thing at night and first thing in the morning. You may need to change it more often on the days when your flow is heaviest.

Don't be tempted to go on wearing the same pad or tampon just because your flow is light. Bacteria can build up and cause an infection (and will also make pads smell a little after a while).

Also, don't use a thicker tampon

PERIOD PANIC — No 3: TAMPONS

Any girl can use a tampon at any age or stage in her life. The walls of the vagina are very flexible and can easily stretch to fit a tampon. (See also "Holey hymen!" on page 47.)

You can't lose a tampon inside yourself. There's nowhere for it to go. It can't slide up past your vagina because the cervix is much too narrow.

It is possible for the string to get tucked up inside your vagina, but in that case you just use your fingers to feel around inside and pull the string back out again. It may sound a bit gross — but it's really no different than putting your fingers inside your own mouth.

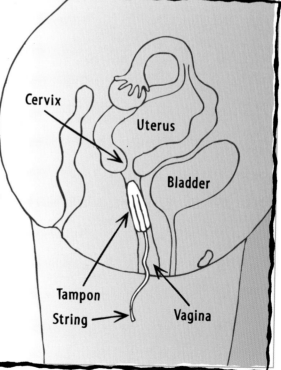

Cervix

Uterus

Bladder

Tampon

String

Vagina

than you need. A thicker tampon won't mean that it will last longer, and it is especially important not to leave tampons in for long stretches of time. Not only is it possible to forget they are there, but wearing too large a tampon or leaving it in for too long can cause a very rare infection — called toxic shock syndrome. *

CHECK IT OUT

Don't flush used pads down the toilet — they block pipes and are bad for the environment. Wrap them in toilet paper or in a bag and put them in the garbage can. You can usually flush tampons down the toilet — but it's better not to.

✳ Toxic shock syndrome is a VERY rare but quite dangerous infection caused by a particular type of bacteria. Symptoms are a high fever, dizziness, headache, vomiting, diarrhea, and a blotchy rash. Take out the tampon and see a doctor as quickly as possible.

▶ **SOME GIRLS WORRY** a lot about how their bodies smell — especially when they have their period. You do have to take a lot more care to keep yourself clean during puberty. As with boys, your body sweats more easily, your

skin and hair are more oily, and you can break out in pimples (see pages 29–30).

But having a period won't make your body smell any more than it normally does. Just make sure you change your sanitary pad regularly, wash your body every day, and wear clean underclothes.

When you wash your vulva, be careful to wash and dry from front to back. Otherwise it's possible to transfer bacteria from your anus into your vagina. It's best to use a plain soap — and stay away from vaginal deodorants as they often irritate this sensitive area.

▶ **BLOOD ISN'T THE** only fluid that comes out of a vagina. Some months before you start having periods, you might find small amounts of a colorless or milky liquid leaking out every now and then, and possibly staining your underpants. This is called a vaginal discharge, and it is usually perfectly healthy and normal.

The fluid comes from glands inside the walls of the vagina. It lubricates the vagina (makes it feel slippery) and helps to keep it healthy. You may find it gets gluey on your panties, and it might smell slightly but it shouldn't smell bad.

However, if your discharge ever becomes heavier or thicker, or changes color and begins to smell nasty, or if your vagina starts to itch a lot or feels sore, you may have a mild infection and need to see a doctor.

▶ **GIRLS DON'T GET** erections like boys do (see page 22), but they do have feelings in their sex organs and these feelings can make them sexually excited. For girls, though, the strongest sensations come from their clitoris.

On the outside...

A girl's outer sex organs are pretty hard to see — even for herself. The best way is to lie on the floor or on your bed, and hold a mirror between your legs. You might feel a bit silly at first but, hey, who's going to see you?

Hand mirror

The external sex organs (vulva)

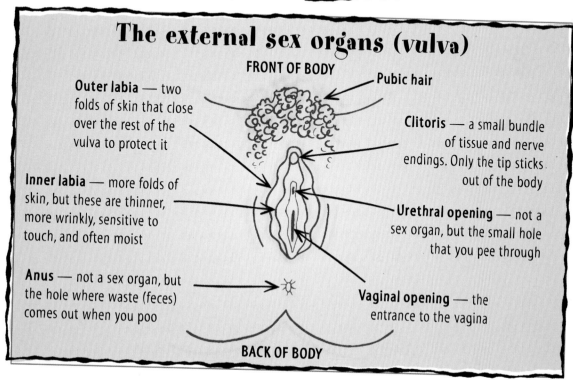

FRONT OF BODY

Pubic hair

Outer labia — two folds of skin that close over the rest of the vulva to protect it

Clitoris — a small bundle of tissue and nerve endings. Only the tip sticks out of the body

Inner labia — more folds of skin, but these are thinner, more wrinkly, sensitive to touch, and often moist

Urethral opening — not a sex organ, but the small hole that you pee through

Anus — not a sex organ, but the hole where waste (feces) comes out when you poo

Vaginal opening — the entrance to the vagina

BACK OF BODY

The clitoris sits right at the front of the vulva. You can only see the tip of it. It's a round fingertip-sized bump underneath the inner labia. The rest of it (which can be up to 4.75 in./12 cm long) is hidden inside the body.

The clitoris is mainly a bundle of nerve endings. It is very sensitive to touch and when rubbed it feels very tingly, pleasurable, and sexy.

The more the clitoris is rubbed, the stronger these feelings become. The clitoris swells up and the vagina makes a lot of fluid and gets very slippery. And, sometimes, the feelings are so strong that a great wave of pleasure rushes right through your body and then dies away. This is called having an orgasm.

▶ **EVEN FROM AN** early age, girls (like boys) can find that touching or rubbing their own sex organs can feel good. After puberty, though, these feelings become much more intense.

Touching yourself like this is called masturbation, and it is a safe and natural way to explore your body and your own sexual responses.

For many girls, having orgasms when they masturbate is trickier at first than it is for boys (see page 24). It can take patience and practice to get to know your clitoris.

46

▶ **MASTURBATION IS** one of those things that almost everyone does, but few people talk about. It is usually a very private and personal act, although mutual masturbation is sometimes done with a partner (see page 71).

Some people feel (either for religious or traditional reasons) that masturbation is not a good thing, but there is nothing unhealthy about it. It isn't harmful and it won't make your hair fall out or mean that you can't have children later on!

It is entirely up to you whether or not you masturbate. If you feel happy about it, that's fine. If you don't, then you don't have to do it.

▶ **AS A YOUNG** adult, it's important to take charge of your body and give it the care and attention it needs. After all, the first person to know if there is something wrong with it will be you.

There is more information about health and health problems in chapter 8, but if you have any worries or concerns about any part of your body — your pimples, breasts, periods, vaginal discharge, anything at all — you need to get proper medical advice.

If you can, talk the problem over first with your mom or dad, or another adult you feel comfortable with. If you can't do that, then no matter how difficult or embarrassing you may think it is, talk to a doctor. Whatever the problem is, they really will have heard it all before, and they will be able to help you.

Holey hymen...!!

The hymen is a thin sheet of skin that stretches across the vaginal opening. It doesn't completely cover the opening and it has holes in it so that your blood can flow out when you have a period.

As you grow, the holes in your hymen get larger and it can break down altogether, especially if you are very active or play lots of sports. Wearing a tampon doesn't damage the hymen, though.

People used to think that an unbroken hymen was a sign that a girl was still a virgin — in other words that she had not had sexual intercourse.

If a girl's hymen hasn't broken naturally, then having sexual intercourse for the first time will break it, and sometimes this causes a little bleeding.

But many girls break their hymens without knowing it, long before they have sex. So whether her hymen is holey or whole, a girl is always a virgin if she has not had sexual intercourse.

A hymen is sometimes called a "cherry" and, when a girl loses her virginity, some people say she's "lost her cherry."

5 | GETTING TO KNOW ... YOU

ACHANGING BODY IS ONE THING, BUT THE EFFECT THAT PUBERTY HAS on your emotions is something else altogether! You start to feel self-conscious — as if all the world is watching you, and waiting for you to do something stupid. You get embarrassed easily and you blush at the drop of a hat! You want people to notice you ... but also

▶ **ONE MINUTE** you're happy or excited, and the next you're angry or feel like crying. And nobody understands what it's like to be you!

Well, you are right. Nobody does, not exactly. But everyone has, or has had, feelings similar to yours at some time in their lives, even your math teacher.

To some extent, all these changing emotions are due to the tidal wave of sex hormones flooding around your body. A sudden change in hormone level can have an enormous effect on how you feel

about yourself and the world, at least until you get used to the new level.

▶ **YOU CAN'T** blame your hormones for everything, though. Puberty is also a time when you start seeing yourself, and other people, in a different way.

You want the world to see you as an individual — as a separate person from your family, with your own ideas about things. Yet at the same time, you still need the support and security your family gives you. It's all part of being in that in-between stage, and it's easy to

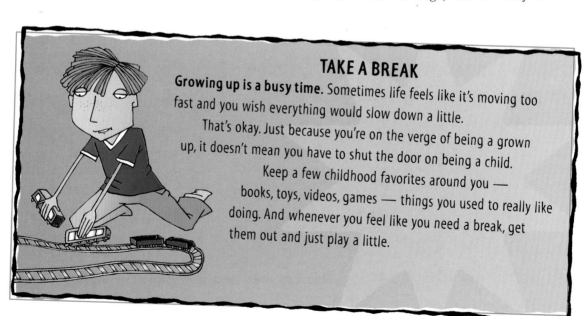

TAKE A BREAK

Growing up is a busy time. Sometimes life feels like it's moving too fast and you wish everything would slow down a little.

That's okay. Just because you're on the verge of being a grown up, it doesn't mean you have to shut the door on being a child.

Keep a few childhood favorites around you — books, toys, videos, games — things you used to really like doing. And whenever you feel like you need a break, get them out and just play a little.

feel confused, upset, or angry with yourself and with everyone around you.

▶ **WHENEVER YOU** feel that things are overwhelming you, try giving yourself some time out. Take a few deep breaths and think about what's happening. Try to see it from another point of view. Is there really a problem or do you just feel like there is?

Maybe you are tired? Tiredness can build up without our realizing it, and there's nothing like lack of sleep to make you feel like the world is out to get you. Have a couple of early nights, or even an occasional afternoon nap!

Believe it or not, exercise is a great stress reliever, too. Being physically active not only takes your mind off whatever is bothering you, it actually has a real effect on your mood by releasing a hormone that makes you feel good.

Keeping a diary or writing things down is another good way of sorting out your feelings. But probably the most helpful thing of all is to talk about it.

The more you bottle something up, the bigger it can seem, so if you keep feeling really down and dismal or you are worried about something, talk it over with someone you trust, like your parents or a good friend. Sharing your problems will help you to feel much less lonely and, you never know, you may get some good advice.

CHECK IT OUT
If you ever feel that you can't talk to your family or any of your friends, try talking to a teacher or a school counselor (or one of the organizations listed at the back of this book).

Your parents are responsible for you until you are 18 years old.

▶ **WHAT IF YOUR** parents are the problem? As children we're happy to let our parents take care of us. They decide what we wear, what we eat, when we go to bed, when we get up, and most of the other things that make up our daily lives. And that's fine — when we are children we need this kind of care.

But as we get older we start having our own opinions about things and it's important to us to have them recognized — whether it's the music we listen to, the color of our bedroom walls, or even the color of our hair.

What do you mean, I can't paint my bedroom black? It's MY room!

▶ **PUBERTY IS** a tough time for every family. No matter how much you love each other you are bound to disagree over something at some time. It's only natural.

But fighting with your family hurts everyone and can lead to years of unhappiness, whereas having their support will make all the other problems of puberty so much easier to deal with. It's worth making an effort to see their point of view, even if it feels like they will never understand yours.

Try to imagine how your parents could be feeling. To them it may seem as if you are rejecting them and everything they stand for. Maybe they feel hurt by your lack of interest in them and the fact that you never seem to want to go anywhere with them, let alone hang around at home.

Plus, no matter how old you are, your parents will always worry about your safety. As you start spending more time outside the home it becomes harder for them to protect you. This makes them feel anxious.

▶ **YOUR PARENTS** need to feel that they can trust you to act responsibly. ∗ You probably feel that your parents should KNOW that you are responsible and should automatically trust you. But what is obvious to you may be far from obvious to them — and shouting at them or slamming your bedroom door isn't going to help.

The key is COMMUNICATION.

Hey, Mom. Is it okay if I'm late getting home from school tonight? Ali's asked me to go look at some CDs with him.

No matter what happens, try to keep talking. If your parents won't listen to you, try talking to another adult who you think they will listen to. Maybe he or she can help you explain how you feel.

You and your parents may never be able to agree on what is best for you, but as long as you go on talking about it you might at least learn to accept each others' differences.

* **Being responsible** means thinking about other people and respecting their feelings. It means knowing right from wrong and not putting yourself or others in danger. It means thinking ahead and not just about what you want.

Parents, who needs them!

You do, so here are some tips for keeping your parents (and yourself) happy.

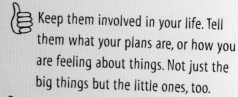 Keep them involved in your life. Tell them what your plans are, or how you are feeling about things. Not just the big things but the little ones, too.

Ask their advice. You don't always have to take it, but listen to what they say, and if you disagree try to explain why.

Accept that they have the right to lay down some rules and try to agree on ones that you both can live with. Be willing to meet them halfway.

Try not to lose your temper, even if you think they are being unreasonable. If you show them that you can accept it when they say no, maybe next time they will be more willing to say yes.

When you want to go out, explain where you want to go and with whom. Agree on a time when you will be back, and ALWAYS let them know if you are going to be late.

Help out more around the house — without waiting to be asked.

Remember, your parents went through puberty, too. Ask them how it was for them. You might be surprised!

▶ **FRIENDS MAKE** all the difference in the world when we're growing up.

Friends understand what we're going through. They listen to our problems, share our worries and concerns, give us advice, introduce us to new ideas, have adventures with us, laugh with us, help us when things go wrong, and generally make us feel like we belong.

In fact, it's easy to feel that your friends are more important than any other part of your life — more important than your family, and especially more important than your schoolwork.

One of the trickiest things about growing up is learning how to juggle the different parts of our lives — such as the things we want for ourselves (hanging out with friends, watching TV, playing on the computer), with the things our families want (regular meals, neat bedrooms,

GIVE AND TAKE

Friendships work best when they are based on mutual respect. In other words, when you all feel much the same way about each other.

If you demand endless support and attention from your friends and don't give any to them in return, they'll soon start feeling resentful and used.

On the other hand, if you let someone make you into a doormat by telling you how to behave and what to do, then you're not being fair to yourself or to them.

visiting relatives), and the things we have to do (going to school, homework).

But balance is what you have to aim for to give yourself as many chances as you can for a happy, successful life.

▶ **MIND YOU,** finding friends isn't always easy. You might start drifting away from the friends you had when you were younger. Or maybe you've moved or transferred to a new school where you don't know anyone and you have to start making friends all over again.

What's more, all of a sudden you find that you start caring what other people think of you — especially people your own age. What you wear, how you look, and who you hang out with all become hugely important.

Nobody likes to be an outsider, but it's easy to start feeling like one — especially if you think that all the other kids you see are cooler or smarter than you, or that they don't seem to have the same worries that you do.

But don't let appearances fool you. Remember, nearly everyone your age has doubts about themselves sometimes; it's just that some people are a lot better at hiding it than others.

Body language

Being confident has a lot to do with looking confident, and looking confident is all about body language.

Think tall. No matter what size you are, if you're feeling insecure it's easy to hunch your shoulders and wrap your arms around yourself. Whenever you find yourself doing this, take a deep breath, unfold your arms, drop your shoulders, and think yourself tall. You'll be amazed at the difference it makes.

Make eye contact. If someone is talking to you, try to look them in the eye. You don't have to stare at them, but looking away from them says that either you think they're boring or you're scared of them!

Keep your hands down. Even if you have a pimple on your nose that's the size of Mount Vesuvius, keep your hands away from your face. Trying to hide it, or any part of your face, with your hands will only draw attention to it. And it goes without saying that playing with your hair, chewing your nails, or sucking your fingers or thumb is a dead giveaway. Sit on your hands if you have to!

▶ **TRY NOT TO LET** shyness and lack of confidence rule your life, even though it sometimes takes a big effort to overcome them.

Build up your confidence by reminding yourself every day of the things you are good at, or that you like about yourself. Don't be too critical. Try to accept that you may never be some of the things you want to be and instead aim for the things you can achieve.

Join an after-school club or an evening class, even if it's something you are only mildly interested in. Or offer your help to a local charity. The main thing is to give yourself as many chances as you can to meet people your own age.

And when you're out and about,

Don't be too possessive. Just because your friends like other people doesn't mean they'll stop being your friends.

don't sit in a corner waiting for everyone else to make the first move. Look around you. Chances are you'll spot a few other people feeling just as lonely or shy as you. Give them a break and go and talk to them. It's hard, but the more often you do it the easier it will get. You don't have to do all the talking. Asking questions is a great way to break the ice.

▶ **NOT FITTING IN** is tough, but try not to pretend to be someone that you aren't just for the sake of belonging. Whether you've got one friend or forty, it's important to believe in yourself.

In any group of friends, some will be more self-confident than others. Mostly this is a good thing, as these people often help the group as a whole to be more adventurous and try out new things. But sometimes one or two people can be so forceful they can take over.

Friendship rules, ok?

A good friend is someone who:

- ↑ Cares about you
- ← Is reliable
- ↓ Doesn't make fun of your weaknesses
- → Gives you good advice
- ↑ Is honest with you
- ← Doesn't try to make you do things you don't want to, or know that you shouldn't
- ↓ Tells you when you are wrong
- → Helps you when you need it
- ↑ Sticks with you through good times and bad
- ← Keeps a secret (as long as it's not harmful to you or someone else)
- ↓ Doesn't get jealous or possessive
- → Helps you feel good about yourself

This isn't so bad if it's just a question of how you dress or what music you play — as long as you are comfortable with it. But sometimes it can lead to more difficult or even dangerous stuff, such as smoking, stealing, or taking drugs.

Groups can also gang up on other kids, and make their lives a nightmare. It is never acceptable to make other people suffer just because they are different than you or your friends — whether they are younger, older, richer, poorer, a different sex, religion, or color, or just go to a different school.

▶ DON'T LET your friends pressure you into doing things that don't feel right to you — no matter what they are. Sticking up for yourself and your own ideas is a vital part of growing up, and doing stuff that you don't want to do will make you miserable.

Try explaining to your friends how you feel. If they make fun of you, or try to make you feel stupid or guilty for not agreeing with them, then they are not good friends. In that case, hard though it may be, it's best to find new friends.

Nope! This just isn't going to work. I need to meet some new people!

'SO, YOU'VE GOT EVERYTHING FIGURED OUT. YOU KNOW ALL ABOUT puberty and, apart from wishing your nose was smaller and you were better at math, you're perfectly happy with yourself and your friends. Then you catch someone's eye across a room. Your stomach flutters, your mouth goes dry, and your palms get sweaty. Either you've got a cold, or you've just discovered "Love!"

▶ **IN FACT, WHAT** you are going through probably has more to do with sex than love at this stage. Your sex drive is gearing up (see page 9), and suddenly you start feeling attracted to people — or to a particular person at least — in a way that you've never been before.

Having a crush on someone means that you think about them all the time.

You're fascinated by them and everything they do, and you want to know all about them. Just thinking about them makes you feel funny inside. You spend hours daydreaming about them and imagining what it would be like to be with them — you might even imagine kissing or cuddling them. In other words, you've got a crush on someone.

▶ **CRUSHES CAN** be huge and totally overwhelming, although they don't often last for very long. The object of your adoration can be almost anyone — from someone famous, like a football player or a film star, to a cool teacher or some other adult you know. Or maybe you're infatuated with a friend's older brother or sister, or even with the kid next door.

He or she might be the opposite sex or the same sex. Girls often have romantic fantasies about older or more glamorous girls or women, and boys can feel the same way about an older boy or man. It doesn't automatically mean that you're gay (see page 59). It doesn't mean you're in love, either. You're just

At least three different hormones act on your body when you have a crush on someone.

Tina, 12, can't stop dreaming about pop star, Brett Powers...

practicing being in love and finding out what it feels like.

But imagining yourself being with someone in a romantic way isn't the same thing as actually doing it. Don't expect the person you have fantasies about to feel the same way about you, especially if they are a lot older than you are.

Forcing your feelings onto someone always leads to disaster, and it is NEVER okay for a child or young person to have any kind of sexual contact with an adult or anyone older than themselves. In fact, it's against the law (see page 85).

Leo, 13, is strangely attracted to the new math teacher...

▶ **HAVING CRUSHES** or sexual daydreams about other people is one of the ways that we learn about our own sexuality. In other words, we find out how we feel about sex — what it means to us, and which of the sexes, male or female, we are most attracted to.

We don't all feel the same way about sex. Some people find it endlessly exciting and fascinating, while others don't think about it much at all — and most of us are somewhere in-between.

Usually, the way we think and feel about sex changes and develops as we get older. Our attitude is affected by lots of things — our own personality, our parents' beliefs and behavior, what we see and hear around us, and our own experiences. Figuring out these thoughts and feelings takes time — sometimes years — and that's perfectly okay.

* **Gay women** are also called lesbians, after the Greek island of Lesbos. A famous woman poet named Sappho lived on Lesbos thousands of years ago, and wrote poems about the ways that women could love each other.

▶ **UNDERSTANDING** which sex you're most attracted to can take time as well. Most adults are attracted to, and feel desire for, people of the opposite sex to themselves. They fall in love with them, have sexual relationships with them, and

Jon, 16, is confused about his friend Ned...

My brother says Ned is ... you know ... one of THEM!

Hi, Jon. Feel like seeing that new Bond movie?

I really like Ned, but if he's gay does that mean I am, too?

make babies with them. These people are called heterosexual or "straight."

But not everyone feels this way. Some men and women are homosexual or "gay."* This means that they are attracted to, and feel desire for, people of the same sex as themselves. They may fall in love with them and have sexual relationships with them, although homosexual couples cannot physically make babies together.

And some people are bisexual. This means that they can be attracted to, and feel desire for, people of either sex.

BEING HOMOSEXUAL or bisexual can be tough … and lonely. Some straight people think that gay people are weird or scary. They may even hate gay people, and make fun of them or physically attack them, just for being gay.

It is never right to hate someone simply because of their sexuality. Despite what some people may say, there is nothing wrong with being gay or bisexual. Your sexuality is a natural part of you and as such it is perfectly normal. Straight, gay, or bisexual, we're all just people.

HOW DO YOU KNOW IF YOU'RE GAY?

Some people know right from the start whether they are gay or not — and some don't.

As well as having a crush on someone of the same sex, we can also feel strong emotions for our friends. Sometimes these emotions have a physical side to them, too. Boys might get erections when they are with other boys, or they might explore masturbation together, and girls might want to kiss or cuddle other girls.

None of this necessarily means that you are gay. Don't rush to put a label on yourself, or on anyone else. Give yourself time and try to discover what your feelings and your body are really telling you. You'll figure it out in the end.

If you do feel sure that you are gay, don't hide it. Talk to someone. Discuss it with your family or a friend if you can. If not, get in touch with an advice group (see pages 104–107). You may not be ready to tell the whole world for a while, but it will be a huge relief to be able to tell someone.

CHECK IT OUT

It's okay for a girl to make the first move. Boys are often much shier than girls and, as long as you don't make a song and dance of it and embarrass him in front of his friends, he'll probably feel very flattered.

▶ **WHETHER YOU** get a crush on someone or not, at some stage you or your friends are going to get interested in dating or "going out."

The problem is, where do you start? It's one thing to hang out with girls or boys who are just friends, but how do you get to know someone when even the sight of them makes you feel tongue-tied and stupid? Well you aren't the only one to feel that way. Even the coolest, most confident people in the world can feel like idiots in front of someone they're attracted to. The thing is not to let your nervousness stop you from trying. (Check out the body language tips on page 53).

Hey Suzy, er ... how did your English exam go?

▶ **PLAN YOUR** approach. Work out what you are going to say beforehand (you could even practice on one of your friends first).

Try to find out what he or she is interested in and use it to start up a conversation. Look for a moment when you're not both surrounded by friends. That way you'll get the chance to talk without worrying what anyone else thinks. Don't be too pushy or aggressive. Keep it casual, but don't be afraid to show that you're interested.

▶ **BE READY** for rejection. No matter how well you plan, sometimes the person you like just won't feel the same way about you. There's not much you can do about that – just accept it and move on.

No one likes being snubbed, or made to look like a fool, but sometimes it happens. If the other person is nervous or unsure of themselves, they might try to hide it by being sarcastic or rude to you.

If so, however hurt or annoyed you feel, keep cool and just chalk it up to experience — and feel good about your own level of maturity.

▶ **IF YOU ARE** asked on a date and you're not too sure how you feel about it, suggest that you go out with a group of friends. That way you can get to know each other without too much pressure.

Take your time. It's easy to worry too much about what you should or should not do on a date. It's natural to want to hold hands with someone you are attracted to, or hug or kiss them, but you ABSOLUTELY don't have to if you don't want to, or don't feel ready to.

And you definitely shouldn't if you are only doing it because all your friends are, or because you think you ought to.

Boys often make the first move just because they think they are expected to. And girls can think that if a boy doesn't want to kiss them on the first date he doesn't like them, so they encourage a boy to kiss them even when they are not sure they really want to.

Try to listen to your feelings and decide what's right for you. Then tell the other person how you feel. Kissing and touching each other should be something you BOTH want to do and no one should make you feel bad for not doing it.

Do you want to kiss?

Um ... not yet. Let's get to know each other a little more, first.

DATING DISASTERS

⊚ Girls sometimes get the giggles when a boy approaches them, or else they try too hard to pretend they're not interested. Both can be a turn-off.

⊚ Boys sometimes think that the best way to show they are interested in a girl is to point her out to their friends, or tease her or make jokes about her. All of which is guaranteed to send the girl running.

⊚ Don't forget to think about how the other person may be feeling. And don't boast about them to your friends.

And remember, your body belongs to you. No one has the right to make you do anything you don't want to do.

▶ **AS YOU START** to feel more comfortable with yourself and with other people, and especially when you are going steady (have a regular boyfriend or girlfriend), you'll want to go a little further with the touchy-feely stuff. This is when things can get tricky.

Moving from simple kissing and holding hands to more serious sexual contact is known as making out or petting, and the trick is knowing when it's okay to do it and how far to go.

▶ **THE ONLY ONE** who can answer those questions is YOU. But before you rush off with the idea that this means you can do anything you want to do, make sure you've got all of the facts first.

Fact number one is: are you sure that your partner feels the same way? Have you asked?

One of you may be more eager to

MALE MYTHS — No. 1: IT'LL BE BAD FOR ME NOT TO

It'll kill me if we don't!

Some girls worry, or are told, that if they start petting with a boy and he gets physically excited (turned on) and has an erection, then it can be harmful to the boy if she wants to stop before he has ejaculated (come).

DON'T BELIEVE IT! It's total nonsense. Certainly the boy may feel disappointed or let down, but it won't make a bit of difference to the state of his health.

If he cares about the relationship, he will hide his disappointment and back off.

push things further than the other. If so, take the time to remember that everyone has the right to say "No" to any kind of sexual contact at any time. And if one of you says "No," the other person has to stop. That's not only the right way to behave, it is also the law (see page 85).

▶ **PETTING, OR** making out, means touching and exploring each other sexually. For example, kissing can move from mouth closed to mouth open. This

Does he want to go further?

Does she want to go further?

Love at first smell? Some scientists think we fall in love with people's smells as much as their looks.

is called "French kissing" and it's when you put your tongue inside the other person's mouth. Touching moves from holding hands or putting your arms around each other, to touching and stroking different parts of the body — especially breasts, nipples, bottoms, thighs, a girl's clitoris or a boy's penis.

▶ **THESE PARTS OF** your body are particularly sensitive, and being touched there can feel so nice that you start getting breathless, tingly, and excited. They are known as your erogenous zones. People can have erogenous zones in other places too. Everyone is different, and part of the fun of a close and loving relationship is discovering where each other's erogenous zones are.

However, being touched anywhere on your body when you don't want to be is not nice or exciting. And if you don't like it you must say so — firmly and clearly.

A girl's clitoris is the most sensitive part of her body. A boy's is his penis.

DRINK, DRUGS, AND SEX

You probably know already that drinking alcohol and taking drugs is incredibly dangerous, especially when you are young. If you haven't been told about the effects of alcohol, or what the different types of illegal drugs are and what they do to you, then you need to find out. Ask your parents, or a teacher — there should be leaflets and books about drinking and the dangers of drug taking in your school or local library.

Aside from what alcohol and drugs can do to your health, the other thing you need to be aware of is the effect they can have on your SEXUAL WELL-BEING.

Alcohol and most drugs lower your inhibitions. This means that they make you forget to be careful, so that you often do things you wouldn't normally do. Sometimes people take them for exactly this reason, and it's also why some people may force them onto others, too.

People often do things they regret when they are drunk or high on drugs. Adults may joke about having hangovers or feeling bad "the morning after." But it's not at all funny if you have forced or have been forced to have sex with someone because you or they were out of control. It's never an excuse, and it 's something you never forget! (See also pages 98–99.)

BOYS SOMETIMES see sex in a different way than girls. They may see it as a challenge. Once they've discovered their own sexuality by masturbating (see page 24), they can be eager to find out how sex works with someone else.

They might be nervous and unsure of themselves, but they may think that the physical side of sex is what it's all about. They can even go the competitive route and start treating sex like some kind of scorecard — checking off the various things they have tried or "levels" they have been able to get to.

They forget, or have not yet realized, that sex has an emotional impact as strong as — sometimes even stronger than — the physical one.

In part, this is due to the rush of hormones urging them on, and to the thrill they feel when they discover how good getting an erection and coming can feel. But it is also because many boys think this is how they should behave.

I thought she was just joking when she said 'No'!

MALE MYTHS — No. 2: GIRLS WHO SAY "NO" DON'T REALLY MEAN IT

This is one male myth that has been around for far too long. It's used by the worst sort of bully. Some boys think that if a girl agrees to go out with him and agrees to some kissing or touching, then she doesn't really mean it when she says she wants to stop.

These boys think the girl just needs persuading to continue. That she's only protesting because he or other people will think she is "easy" if she doesn't.

But no matter how much petting they have done, or how many other boys the girl has been out with, or how she is dressed, or how much money he has spent on their date — it is NEVER okay for a boy to force a girl into any kind of sexual contact. It is against the law, and it could lead to a charge of ATTEMPTED RAPE or even RAPE — see pages 98–99.

Books, magazines, movies, and things they hear from other, often older, boys make them think that they are supposed to get as much experience as they can, as quickly as they can — sometimes without thinking too much about who they are getting that experience with!

▶ GIRLS OFTEN CARE much more about the emotional side of sex. They might be just as curious about the physical things that people do and what they feel like, but they also want to feel admired and cared for, even loved.

Girls don't usually respond as quickly as boys to physical stimulation — being touched or stroked on their sex organs and other parts of their body — even when they are doing it themselves (see page 46). They need to feel relaxed about themselves and confident of the person they are with.

But sometimes the urge to be emotionally important to someone (to have a boyfriend) is so strong, girls make the mistake of thinking that they can trade physical experiences for emotional ones. In other words, that if they let a boy touch them, and pretend to enjoy it, the boy will like them more.

▶ THIS ISN'T A GOOD situation for either person. It's wrong to lead someone on, for whatever reason. The more time you spend together the harder it is to fake feelings that you don't have. Eventually you will both feel cheated

and unhappy, and you could even end up hating each other.

Of course, there are also lots of boys who need to feel just as emotionally involved as their partners. And, sadly, there are some girls who also fall into the trap of being sexual competitors.

MALE MYTHS — No. 3: BOY VIRGINS ARE WIMPS

Some teenage boys see sex and sexual experiences as a sort of race. The "winners" are those who lose their virginity (have sexual intercourse) fairly early on — the "losers" are those who don't.

By the time a boy reaches his mid-teens he might be teased by other boys if he admits to not having much sexual experience. So ... lots of boys lie about it. Then other boys panic because THEY think they are the only ones who don't have any experience, and so it goes on.

The problem is, this kind of worry is what makes boys rush off to have sex with anyone who will let them, just so they can impress their friends.

They won't impress the girls, though. In fact many girls are relieved to discover that their boyfriend is still a virgin. It makes their relationship so much more special and they feel less pressure on them to do things they may not be ready to do.

I've had hundreds!

Well, I've had thousands!

We like taking things slowly!

SO WHAT'S wrong with petting? Well, as long as you like the person you are doing it with, take things slowly, and are careful and thoughtful of each other, then there's nothing wrong with it. It is completely natural to want to explore your own and someone else's sexuality.

Sooner or later, though, petting leads to one big question — do you or don't you do IT? Doing it, or going all the way, both mean one thing — having sexual intercourse.

The physical side of what sexual intercourse is, and how to protect yourself and your partner against an unwanted pregnancy or a sexually transmitted infection, is covered in detail in the next two chapters. It's vital to know this information, BUT it's also vital to know and understand the emotional impact of having sexual intercourse.

REASONS NOT TO HAVE SEX

If you are wondering whether or not to have intercourse with someone, ask yourself if your reason for doing it might be one or other of the following — and if it is, think again.

- ✖ Because your boyfriend or girlfriend wants you to.
- ✖ Because you think everyone else is doing it.
- ✖ To prove how much you love someone.
- ✖ Because you think it will make you more grown up.
- ✖ Because you think it will make someone love you.
- ✖ Because you think your girlfriend or boyfriend will dump you if you don't.

- ✖ Because you're curious and want to know what it's all about.
- ✖ Because you're bored or lonely.
- ✖ So you can tell all your friends.
- ✖ Because you're afraid of hurting the other person's feelings.
- ✖ Because you think it will make you popular, or cool.
- ✖ Because you want to get the whole "Do I, don't I?" question over with.
- ✖ Because you don't know how to say "No" (see next page).

▶ **WHEN YOU HAVE** any kind of sexual contact with someone, you are letting them get close to you in ways that no other person can.

When you love and trust each other, this closeness or intimacy gives you a wonderful, warm feeling. You feel great about yourself, you feel great about the person, and the world becomes a fabulous place to be.

When you have sexual contact with someone you don't love or trust (at least, not in a sexual way), the opposite is true. You feel bad about yourself, you feel bad about them, and the world becomes a difficult and very hard place to be.

If you loved me you would.

You're going to do it some time, so why not now?

It'll clear up your skin.

Don't be such a baby, everyone else is doing it.

SAYING NO

It's not always boys who put on the pressure when it comes to sex — sometimes girls want or expect more from their boyfriends than the boys feel ready for. In both cases, saying "No" can be hard to do.

You might feel too embarrassed to talk about it, or worried that you would look like a fool. You might be scared that your boyfriend or girlfriend will think you are being childish or uptight and won't want to be with you anymore. Girls, especially, find it difficult to say "No," in case they hurt the boy's feelings. Sometimes it can seem easier just to let it happen.

DON'T!

If you're not absolutely 100 percent sure that you want something to happen, you must say "No" as firmly and as clearly as possible. If you don't, you'll end up disliking yourself and feeling that you've let yourself down.

✘ NO, slow down. You're going too fast for me.

✘ NO, we don't know each other well enough.

✘ NO, if you cared about me you'd stop hassling me.

✘ NO, there's more to having a relationship than sex.

✘ **NO, I JUST DON'T WANT TO, AND THAT'S THAT!**

What's the matter, don't you trust me?

You won't get pregnant, honest.

We'll only do it once.

If you won't, I'll find someone who will!

YOU DON'T HAVE TO KEEP ON DOING IT

Even if you do have intercourse with someone, don't think that you have to keep on doing it if you don't want to. If it has left you feeling unhappy or bad about yourself, tell the other person how you feel.

You don't have to make it sound like it's their fault, but explain to them that you've realized that you aren't ready for a full sexual relationship yet.

Your partner may be disappointed or hurt, but if they care about you they will respect your feelings and not put pressure on you to change your mind.

It's okay, I don't feel ready yet either!

▶ **ASIDE FROM** giving birth, sexual intercourse is the closest we can ever physically get to another person. So it makes sense that the feelings it gives us are so powerful — both the good ones and the bad. It takes some maturity (some understanding of ourselves and the world) before we are really able to handle such strong emotions, and deal with the things that can happen as a result of having intercourse.

I don't really want a sexual relationship yet!

I do!

Becoming mature takes time and, if we're honest about it, most of us realize that we aren't really mature enough to handle intercourse until at least our late teens, when the worst effects of puberty are starting to settle down.

▶ **SEX AND LOVE** aren't the same thing. Remember those hormones? Our bodies want us to have sex so we can make babies — that's what our sex organs are for. So our bodies produce hormones that make us want to have sex. And the closer we get to having intercourse, the more those hormones encourage us to go all the way!

Wanting to have sex is known as sexual desire, and it is so strong it can make us behave in ways that we normally wouldn't. It can make us think we want to have sex with someone when we don't even know them very well, let alone love them. And that can be a disaster.

Mark, 17, finds a perfect relationship with Naomi...

This is GREAT. We've got so much in common!

It's so easy to talk to you, Naomi, you really understand.

I could just go on kissing forever...

▶ **THERE'S SO MUCH** written and said about sex, it's easy to think it's the biggest thing going in a relationship.

People confuse the physical closeness of sex with the kind of closeness that comes from knowing someone really well. But having sex is no substitute for just spending time with each other.

Good relationships are built on enjoying each other's company. They're about friendship and having fun together, sharing plans and ideas, trusting each other, giving each other help and support, and getting involved in each other's lives, friends, and families.

Once you start having sex in a relationship, it can take over and become the most important part of it. It can even become the only thing you do together. When that happens, at least one of you is going to get bored and miserable.

▶ **HAVING SEX** too soon can leave you with bad memories and a bad feeling about yourself. First-time sex often isn't a wonderful thing. It can be awkward and embarrassing, and might well leave you wondering what all the fuss was about.

Having good sex with someone takes time, and is best with someone you really care about and feel committed to. If you break up with someone after you've had sex, it can make the hurt and rejection you feel even harder to bear. You can end up feeling used and secondhand.

▶ **THERE ARE LOTS** of things you can do for each other in a happy and secure sexual relationship without actually having sexual intercourse.

With care and thoughtfulness (and a little imagination), you can find other ways to please and excite each other.

▶ **SERIOUS OR** heavy petting is also known as foreplay, because often it comes before intercourse. But foreplay can be enjoyable in itself, and can lead to orgasm for both partners without having intercourse. (In fact, few girls have orgasms through sexual intercourse alone; often they need to have their clitoris touched at the same time — but make sure you read the Check it Out box on page 74.)

Foreplay includes mutual masturbation — rubbing and stroking each other's penis or clitoris. It also includes oral sex, when one or both partners use their mouth and tongue to kiss and lick their partner's penis or clitoris. BUT don't feel you have to have oral sex if you don't want to. Not everyone enjoys it and that's fine. (Also, make sure you read about HIV/AIDS on page 97.)

Above all, remember that there are lots of ways to show you love someone – having sex is only ONE of them.

WHAT MAKES A GOOD RELATIONSHIP?

You can be attracted to someone in an instant, but a good relationship takes time and patience. For example, do you both:

- ✓ Share your thoughts and ideas
- ✓ Respect each other's opinions
- ✓ Share the same sense of humor
- ✓ Trust each other
- ✓ Try not to be jealous or possessive
- ✓ Know when to admit you are wrong
- ✓ Accept each other's faults
- ✓ Show kindness to each other
- ✓ Do fun things together
- ✓ Give each other support
- ✓ Listen to each other's problems
- ✓ Help each other out
- ✓ Try to be patient with each other
- ✓ Accept each other's friends and family

7 HOW SEX GETS YOU PREGNANT

OKAY, I KNOW YOU GET TAUGHT THIS AT SCHOOL AND MAYBE YOU know all about it already, but let's just go through it one more time. Because, believe me, there are lots of unhappy kids out there who either fell asleep during the important parts, or somehow thought it didn't apply to them. But it did …

> ## It's a fact!
> **You or your partner could get pregnant …**
>
> ▶ Anytime you have sexual intercourse and in any way — even if you are using some sort of birth control or contraception (see chapter 8).
> ▶ The first time you have sex.
> ▶ If you have sex during your (or your partner's) monthly period.
> ▶ If you have sex before you (or your partner) have started having periods — you (or she) might be about to start and it's impossible to know beforehand.
> ▶ If you have sex standing up.
> ▶ If you have sex without an orgasm.
> ▶ If you or your partner withdraws (pulls out of the vagina) before ejaculating — see page 89.
> ▶ If the vagina is washed right after having sex.
> ▶ YOU CAN EVEN GET PREGNANT IF YOU DON'T ACTUALLY HAVE INTERCOURSE — see the Check It Out box on page 74.

▶ **WHEN TWO PEOPLE** have sexual intercourse, the man puts his erect penis inside the woman's vagina. (The muscley walls of the vagina are very elastic, and stretch to fit the penis.) Then one or both partners move their hips so that the penis slides back and forth inside the vagina, rubbing against the vaginal walls.

This feels very pleasurable to the man (and often to the women too, although there is a lot less feeling inside the vagina than in the clitoris.)

Eventually, but not always, these feelings build up until the man ejaculates semen into the woman's vagina. Once he has ejaculated, the man's penis gradually returns to its normal size and slides out of the woman's vagina. And that's basically it.

Except, of course, that it isn't …

CHECK IT OUT
Having sex won't make you or your partner pregnant EVERY time you do it, but it's the ONE time it does that matters!

An ejaculation of just a few teaspoonfuls of semen can contain anything from 200 to 500 million sperm.

Sperm can survive for up to five days inside a woman's body, but many of them don't. Two-thirds of them don't even make it as far as the fallopian tubes, and half of those will choose the wrong tube. (There's usually only one egg in one of the tubes at any one time, remember. *)

AS SOON AS semen gets into the vagina the millions of sperm it carries begin a life-or-death race through the cervix and the womb to the fallopian tubes. (If you haven't read them yet, chapters 3 and 4 tell you what all these parts are.)

Like microscopic, heat-seeking missiles, each sperm is searching for an egg — and it's a race against the clock.

* Every once in a while, two eggs are released into the fallopian tubes at the same time. If BOTH are fertilized by sperm, twin babies can form. They won't be identical twins, as they came from different eggs. Identical twins only happen when a fertilized egg divides and two babies form from a single egg.

If there's no egg in the tube, the sperm die within 48 hours of getting there. But if there is an egg, the sperm push and prod at its outer layers in the hope that one of them will be able to get through.

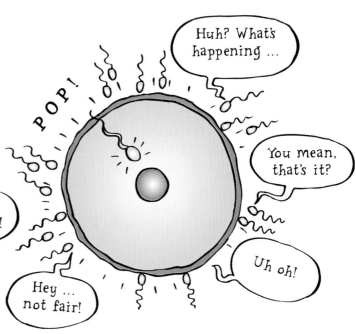

If one sperm does get inside, the egg immediately puts out a chemical barrier to keep the rest away. All the other sperm are locked out and die.

HOW DO YOU KNOW IF YOU'RE PREGNANT?
As soon as a fertilized egg attaches itself to the wall of the womb, changes start taking place in your body.

[!] You stop having periods. If you miss a period, or your period arrives but is very patchy and light, this could be the first sign that you are pregnant.

[!] Your breasts may feel swollen and sore.

[!] You might find that you suddenly don't want foods or drinks that you liked before, and/or that you have a strange taste in your mouth.

[!] You might feel sick or queasy, especially first thing in the morning.

[!] You might feel very tired.

[!] You may need to urinate more than usual.

If you think you may be pregnant, you'll need to do a pregnancy test. Most doctors and family planning clinics do these for free. You can buy a kit from a pharmacy, but if the test is positive you should see your doctor. If it's negative but your period still doesn't arrive, also see your doctor.

▶ **FOR THE ONE** lucky sperm, though, it's just the beginning. Both eggs and sperm are cells — the tiny building blocks from which all living things are made. But they are different than any other kinds of cell. They each hold only half the information that every cell carries about the body it belongs to.

This information is held in a part of the cell called the nucleus. When the egg cell and the sperm cell join up, the two nuclei instantly lock together — like two halves of a puzzle — to make one complete cell.

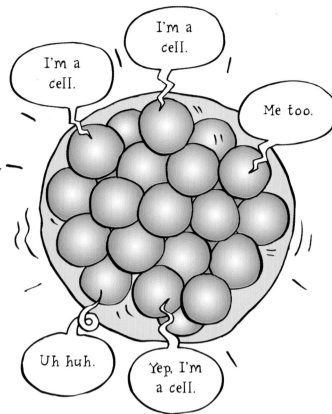

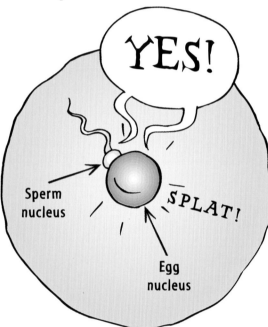

▶ **NEXT, THE ONE** complete cell divides to make two complete cells … the two cells divide to make four … the four divide to make eight … and so it goes. As the fertilized egg drifts on down the fallopian tube, it is growing, and growing all the time.

It takes an egg about three days to get to the end of a fallopian tube. By this time, the fertilized egg has become a ball of about 16 cells. For another day or two, the ball of cells floats in the womb, making more cells all the time. Then it fixes itself to the wall of the womb and stays there. *

* Sometimes the ball of cells comes away from the side of the womb, or it fails to fix itself properly. When this happens the pregnancy comes to an end. Bleeding starts and the ball of cells is carried out of the body with the blood. This is called a miscarriage.

▶ **IN THE HEART** of the cell ball, the dividing cells are forming an embryo — a tiny clump of life. Over the next few weeks, the embryo develops a head, arms, legs, eyes, nose, and ears, and starts to look vaguely human.

After eight weeks, the embryo is almost complete — a miniature baby less than 1 inch (3 centimeters) long. From now on it is called a fetus, and it will grow rapidly in size and weight until it is born about 30 weeks later.

As the fetus grows, the mother gains in size and weight, too, and her breasts swell in readiness for the baby's birth.

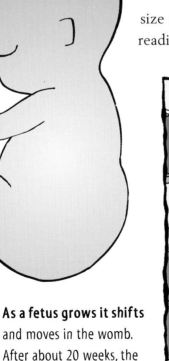

As a fetus grows it shifts and moves in the womb. After about 20 weeks, the mother can feel her baby moving around inside her.

WHEN A BABY is ready to be born, it is usually upside down, with its head pointing toward the vagina. The muscley walls of the womb start to tense and relax in waves called contractions.

Nearly there ... just one more push should do it ...

The cervix stretches until it is about 4 inches (10 centimeters) across. When the cervix is wide enough, the contractions slowly push the baby through the cervix and out of the vagina. Once the baby's head is through, the rest of its body slides out pretty quickly.

HOWEVER, NOT all births happen quite in that way. Sometimes the baby doesn't turn head-down in the womb and decides to come out feet first, instead. This is known as a breech birth and it needs the help of a specially trained nurse or doctor.

Some babies just can't manage to get through the cervix and vagina at all on their own. When this happens, the doctor carefully cuts through the wall of the mother's belly, lifts the baby out, then sews up the cut. This is called a Caesarean birth (after the famous Roman general Julius Caesar, who was supposed to have been born in a similar way).

Today, Caesarean births are regularly carried out in hospitals, and many babies are born in this way.

ANYONE, MALE OR female, who has ever been there when a baby is born knows what a heart-stoppingly exciting and wonderful event it is. The rush of feeling you have for a newborn baby when it is handed to you can overwhelm even complete strangers.

This is a new life and it demands, and has a right to, care, protection, and most of all love.

Isn't she just amazing?

Yeah ... and so are you!

But caring for a baby is hard work! Babies need constant, 24-hour attention. Even when they are asleep, someone needs to be close by at all times. Babies have to be fed, clothed, washed, changed, played with, and cuddled, over and over again, day after day.

They need special clothes, special food, special medicines, and somewhere clean and safe to sleep and play.

> I thought babies were supposed to sleep a lot?

> Yeah ... just not necessarily at nighttime.

▶ **EVEN WITH** the help of a loving and supportive family, bringing up a baby isn't easy. For teenage parents, who have barely begun to live their own lives, it can be almost impossibly tough. And a baby is just the beginning — any child you have will be your responsibility for the next 18 YEARS!

The best solution is — DON'T GET PREGNANT — at least, not until you are old enough to be sure that you're doing the right thing.

▶ **BUT WHAT IF** you do get pregnant — what then? Well, then you need to get help — fast! Whatever you do, don't try to hide it and hope that it will just go away. It won't!

> If I don't tell anyone, maybe my period will come back ...

No matter how hard it may be, tell your parents. They can help you, and you will need their help.

Even though they may be shocked or angry at first, they will also be HUGELY relieved that you have told them, and given them the chance to give you their advice and support while you decide what you want to do about it.

It will also be an enormous relief to you to know that you don't have to try to hide it from them.

WITH OR WITHOUT your parents you should see a doctor as quickly as possible. Your doctor will confirm whether or not you really are pregnant, and will give you advice about how to take care of yourself and what you need to do next. If you can't face seeing your own family doctor, go to a family planning or prenatal care center. See pages 104–107 for some useful places to contact.

You should also tell the boy who made you pregnant — even if you don't know him very well. Hopefully he will want to give you whatever help and support he can, but even if he doesn't (or even if you don't want him to), he should know what has happened (if only so that he is more careful in the future).

> Um ... I'm going to have a baby, and you're the father!

When you tell your boyfriend that you're pregnant, try to do it calmly and remember to give him time to get over the shock.

YOU NEED TO decide what you are going to do. It really comes down to three choices, and you must think carefully about each one. Your decision will affect more lives than just your own!

1 You could have the baby and bring it up in whatever way you can. If you and your partner are both over the age of 16 and have a strong, loving relationship, you might decide that you want to live together or perhaps get married (with parental permission) and bring up the baby together.

However, if you are both below the

CHECK IT OUT
Some girls think that if they are a single parent, social services will give them an apartment to live in and money to support themselves and their child. In fact, many single parents are desperately poor and live in very difficult conditions!

age of 18, this is not likely to be possible without the support of your families.

If you don't want to marry or live with the father, then perhaps your family will let you stay at home and help you raise your child on your own.

But if your parents can't (or won't) help you, then you have to think about where you will live and how you will earn enough money to support yourself and your child in the future.

WHAT IF YOU ARE THE FATHER?

The news that you've made a girl pregnant will probably hit you like a 10-ton truck!

You'll be shocked, horrified ... and scared to death! Your first thought may even be "Hey! it's got nothing to do with me!" But think again.

Even if you never see the girl again, if she decides to keep the baby, you could find yourself having to help to support her and your child by sending them money every month for the next 18 years!

However, once you've gotten over the shock, you might find that your feelings about fathering a child are a lot more complicated than "nothing to do with me!"

Don't worry, I'll help you, whatever you decide to do!

Whatever those feelings are, you need to know that legally you have no rights over the girl's decision about whether she has the baby, has an abortion, or has the baby adopted.

Of course, this doesn't mean that you can't let her know how you feel about it, or that you can't help her to make her decision. But try not to add to the pressure she will be feeling, and do think carefully about what will be best for her and for your child — not just what will be best for you!

If she does decide to keep the baby, you will then have both the right and the responsibility of being involved in your child's upbringing.

I've found the perfect couple to take care of your baby. I'm sure he will be very happy with them.

2. If you want to have the baby but feel that you are not old enough or are not able to bring up your child yourself, then you could give the baby up for adoption. In this case, you should talk it over with an adoption agency or social services adviser — see pages 104–107.

There are lots of older couples with secure and comfortable homes who are desperate to adopt and raise a child. Sadly, though, most prefer to adopt young babies, so the earlier this decision is made the better it is for the baby.

BE WARNED!
NEVER, EVER attempt to give yourself an abortion, or get an illegal abortion from someone who is not a licensed doctor.
IT COULD KILL YOU!

3 You may feel emotionally and/or physically unable to face going ahead with the pregnancy, in which case you need to talk to a doctor about getting a termination, or abortion.

An abortion is the process by which an embryo or fetus is removed from the womb. If the abortion happens within the first eight weeks, it can often be done by taking a special pill. Otherwise it must be done surgically. Most abortions are carried out within the first 12 weeks of a pregnancy. After that, many doctors are unhappy about doing it unless there are strong medical reasons for it.

I just don't think I can face having a baby!

▶ **THE LAWS ON** abortion vary depending on where you live. In the United States and Canada, for example, abortions are legal as long as they meet certain conditions. In the United States, the rights and restrictions related to abortion are governed by state law.

You will usually need more than one doctor to agree that an abortion is necessary. And, if you are under 18, you may need permission from a parent or guardian before the abortion can be performed. However, you cannot be made to have an abortion if you don't want one, even if you are under 18.

Some people think that abortion is an easy solution to an unwanted pregnancy — until they are faced with such a decision themselves. It may be a necessary solution, but it is never an easy one. Both partners can feel achingly sad and guilt-ridden and,

for the girl at least, the feelings of sorrow and loss may stay with her all her life.

▶ **THESE ARE ALL** difficult choices to make, and the right answer will be different for everyone. You will need advice — and will probably get lots of it. You may even face pressure from your parents, your partner, your friends, or possibly your teacher or a religious adviser, to do one thing or another.

It is vitally important that you don't let yourself be pushed into doing something that you don't really want to do — whatever it is. In the end, only you can truly understand how you feel about yourself, your future, and your pregnancy. And only you have the right to make a decision that will be yours for the rest of your life.

8 A SURVIVAL GUIDE...

THIS CHAPTER HAS ALL THE HEAVY STUFF IN IT — THE STUFF YOU really NEED to know — like how ***not*** to get yourself (or someone else) pregnant, how ***not*** to get a sexually transmitted disease (STD), and ***how*** to keep yourself safe and healthy. ***Read and remember!***

▶ **YOUR BODY IS** yours. You own it, it belongs to you, and no one has the right to make you do anything with it or to it that you don't want to do. But along with the right to own your body comes the responsibility for looking after it.

That doesn't just mean eating the right sort of food or getting enough sleep at night (although these kinds of things are important as well). It means understanding that what you do with your body can be harmful to you, and taking care not to put yourself, or others, at risk.

▶ **RULE NUMBER ONE** is ... if ever you think there is even the smallest, slightest, most remote chance that you might have sex with somebody, make sure you are both protected — not only from an unwanted pregnancy, but also from the possibility of getting a sexually transmitted disease (STD).

STD (also known as STI, for sexually transmitted infection) is the general name given to a group of illnesses you can get by having sexual intercourse or, in some cases, by heavy petting. (See pages 93–97 for more info on STDs.)

You can protect yourself or your partner from getting pregnant in a number of different ways — mostly by using some type of contraceptive. *

But, if you have sex, there is ONLY ONE WAY of avoiding a STD, and that's by using a condom.

> ***Contraceptives** are things you use for preventing pregnancy. The word contraception comes from two words put together. Contra means "against" in Latin, and conception means getting pregnant.

> Yeah, sure ... I knew that ... ???

SEX AND THE LAW

Just as there are laws about drinking alcohol and taking drugs, there are laws about sexual behavior, too. Most places have similar sorts of laws and they are there to protect you.

▦ In the United States, state law determines the legal age at which you can have sex. Generally, the ages range from 16 to 18 and may require parental consent. The legal age at which you can have sex is known as the age of consent. Check the law for your state to find out if you are under the age of consent.

Even if both partners have agreed to have sex, the boy or man can be prosecuted (taken to court) and sent to prison if the girl is below the age of consent. Girls are not prosecuted for under-age sex.

▦ Laws related to homosexual sex (male or female) also vary from state to state. Some states regard homosexual sex as illegal at any age and some states have no current law on the age of consent. Generally, in those states that have an age of consent law for male (and female) homosexual sex, the age ranges from 16 to 18. Check the law in your state.

▦ It is not against the law to be given advice about contraception under the age of 16, or to own or buy methods of contraception. There are no age restrictions on buying condoms.

▦ The age at which you can get married with or without parental consent is determined by state law. Generally, you can get married at age 16 with parental consent and at age 18 without parental consent. Check the law for your state.

＊ **In Canada** the age at which people can legally have sex is 14 for both heterosexual and female homosexual couples. The legal age of consent for male homosexual couples is 18. Each province has its own laws about the age requirements for marriage, so check the law for your province.

▶ **A CONDOM IS** like a tight-fitting sock that's rolled onto a penis so that the penis is completely covered. It has to be put on before the penis goes into the vagina, and it acts like a barrier between the penis and the vaginal walls. At the "toe end" most condoms have a shaped tip or teat for catching the sperm during an ejaculation. This stops the sperm from getting into the vagina.

A condom has to be rolled on when the penis is erect — otherwise it's impossible to get it on. It also slides off very easily once the penis goes limp and starts to shrink back to its normal size.

Most condoms are made of very thin, stretchy latex or polyurethane, with a lubricant (a slippery coating) on the

OTHER WORDS FOR
Condom — rubber, glove, hat, sock

* Spermicides
also exist as creams, gels, or foam and can be used as extra protection inside the vagina, or around the outside of a condom once it is on. They **don't** work just on their own, though.

inside that makes them easier to put on. The lubricant may also contain a spermicide — a chemical that kills sperm. * Condoms are made from other materials, too, but only latex or polyurethane condoms stop germs from passing through them, so the other types aren't much use against STDs.

Condoms are sold in all kinds of places — in pharmacies, supermarkets, newsstands, gas stations, and from vending machines in public toilets — and anyone can buy them at any age. You can also get them free from family planning advice centers (see pages 104–107).

So they're cheap, easy to get, fairly easy to use (once you've got the hang of it), aren't harmful to your health and, if

Those toilets were horrible!

Yes, but did you get them?

CONDOMANIA

Learn this list by heart! Condoms only work when they are used properly.

→ **DO** make sure that the condom is made of latex or polyurethane.

→ **DON'T** use a condom after the "use by" date on its packaging. Like everything, condoms decay with age. Using an out-of-date condom means that it could tear at the worst possible moment.

→ **DON'T** use a condom more than once.

→ **DON'T** use a condom if the wrapper has been opened, or if the condom has been unrolled, or is sticking to itself.

→ **DON'T** let an erect penis get near the vagina before putting on a condom. Small amounts of semen can leak out of a penis long before ejaculation.

→ **DO** be careful not to puncture or poke holes in the condom with your nails when putting it on.

→ **DO** put a WATER-based cream or jelly (with or without a spermicide in it) on the condom once it's on the penis. It helps the penis slide in and out of the vagina without tearing the condom.

→ **DON'T** put any kind of OIL-based lubricant on a condom, as this could damage the material.

→ **DO** make sure you hold on to the condom when the penis slides out of the vagina. Otherwise the condom could slip off and semen might leak into the vagina.

used properly EVERY time you have sex, they will do a pretty good job of preventing pregnancy and infection.

That's it, then, problem solved, right? Nope, sadly, it's not!

▶ THE BIG PROBLEM with condoms

is that boys (and girls) are often too embarrassed to use them! They would rather just hope that nothing bad is going to happen to them. Hmmm … doesn't sound like such a great idea, does it?

● Part of the reason for this is that we tend to see intercourse as a big romantic event. A condom seems too practical, too obvious, too uncool — and about as romantic as your grandma's false teeth.

● Both boys and girls worry that if they have a condom with them, their partner will think they have planned to have sex all along.

● Boys worry that they won't be able to put the condom on properly and will end up looking stupid.

● Girls worry that they won't know what to do if the boy asks them to put it on him.

● Boys and girls find it awkward or embarrassing to stop what they and their partner are doing in order to get out a condom.

● Boys worry that their erection may go before they can get the condom on.

● Girls feel too shy to argue when a boy tells them not to worry and promises not to come inside them.

● Neither partner has talked to the other one about contraception or about protection from STDs and doesn't know how to begin.

▶ AFTER ALL, let's face it, condoms

are pretty silly looking … and it is embarrassing suddenly to leap into a

CHECK IT OUT

There is a type of condom designed for girls to wear. Female condoms work in much the same way as male ones except that they line the inside of the vagina, so they are wider and have a bendy ring at both ends to hold them in place. The problem is making sure that they don't slip out of place, and that the penis goes inside the condom and doesn't push it to one side. They are also not as easy to buy as male condoms and they are more expensive.

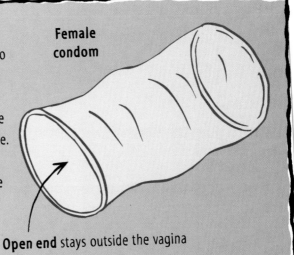

Female condom

Open end stays outside the vagina

conversation about them. But, without making too big a fuss about it ...

USING A CONDOM COULD SAVE YOUR LIFE!!!

And if you think I'm kidding, check out the info on HIV/AIDS on page 97!

But remember, condoms are NOT foolproof. They can slip off during intercourse, so it's a good idea to check with your fingers now and then to make sure that the rim of the condom is still at the base of the penis. Also, condoms are so thin they can split or tear. (See Emergency Contraception on page 92.)

▶ **A LAST WORD** on condoms. No matter how necessary they are, some men (and boys) say that they won't wear condoms because having sex doesn't feel as good with a condom on.

The only answer to this is that if they are not mature enough to understand the importance of keeping themselves and their partners safe — then they are not mature enough to have sex!

It is true that there are a few (but only a few) men who are allergic to condoms and get a red itchy rash from wearing them. But it is possible to buy condoms that are specially designed not to cause an allergic rash.

▷ Putting on a condom...

Don't wait until it's too late — find out for yourself what condoms are like and how they work, even if you know FOR SURE that you are never, ever going to have sex with anyone! ✱

Take a packet home and practice in your bedroom or bathroom. At least it will be one less thing to worry about.

1 Carefully tear along one side of the individual packet so you don't damage the condom inside. The condom will be rolled up. Make sure the tip is sticking up on the inside of the ring and the roll of latex is on the outside.

2 Before you start unrolling it, gently squeeze the closed end (the tip) of the condom between your finger and thumb to make sure there is no air trapped inside it. A trapped air bubble could cause the condom to split.

✱**Girls — this means you, too.** If you know what a condom looks and feels like, it will be less awkward and embarrassing for both of you when the big moment comes.

CONDOMS ARE a contraceptive, but there are other ways of avoiding pregnancy (remember, though, that ONLY condoms protect you from STDs).

The absolutely best method of all is not to have intercourse — at least, not until you feel sure you are in a lasting relationship and are able and ready to discuss contraception with your partner.

The absolutely worst method is the "withdrawal" method. This means pulling out, or withdrawing, the penis from the vagina just before ejaculation happens.

No matter what anyone says, this is pretty useless! An erect penis often leaks drops of liquid called preseminal fluid. Preseminal fluid can carry sperm. And,

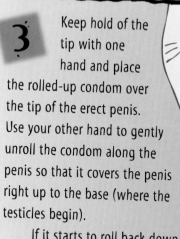

3 Keep hold of the tip with one hand and place the rolled-up condom over the tip of the erect penis. Use your other hand to gently unroll the condom along the penis so that it covers the penis right up to the base (where the testicles begin).

If it starts to roll back down, simply roll it up again. If the condom unrolls fully and slips off, start again with another condom.

4 After ejaculation, and before the penis has relaxed, carefully pull the penis out of the vagina, making sure the condom stays in place. Only take the condom off when the penis is well away from your partner's vagina.

Wrap used condoms in tissue and put them in a garbage can — NOT down the toilet. They block drains and are bad for the environment.

DO NOT USE A CONDOM MORE THAN ONCE!

in the excitement of the moment, it's often difficult (if not impossible) for a boy or man to pull out in time.

Then there's the "natural" or "rhythm" method. This relies on working out which days are safe for intercourse, and which aren't, based on where a girl or woman is in her monthly period cycle.

In fact, this is fairly useless too, as there are no really safe days. A woman's egg-producing cycle changes from month to month, and it is almost impossible to know exactly when it is going to happen.

▶ **FOR ALL OTHER** forms of contraception you need to go to a doctor, or a family-planning center (see pages 104–107). You can get advice and contraceptives without your parents' consent — but, if you can, it's a good idea to try at least to talk about it with your parents first.

▶ **DIAPHRAGMS OR CAPS** work a bit like female condoms. They are flat, round, cap-like objects made of a thicker rubber than condoms, and with a bendy rubber rim. They are pushed up inside the vagina until they fit over the cervix at the very top.

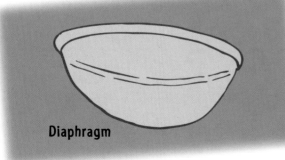

Diaphragm

> Now, let's see. What's your opinion of the diaphragm?

Don't leave it to luck: if you are thinking of having sex, discuss contraception BEFOREHAND!

Caps are used with spermicides, and you have to be taught how to put one in properly. You also need to be fitted for the right size of cap.

They can be put in a few hours before intercourse and must be left in place for a few hours afterward. Then they are taken out and washed so they can be used again.

▶ **THE CONTRACEPTIVE PILL** comes in all sorts of different types and varieties, but they all belong to one of two groups — the combined pill and the progestogen-only pill (progestogen is a type of progesterone). Both groups contain artificially produced hormones.

In the combined pill, the hormones stop a woman's eggs from maturing, so her ovaries don't release any eggs. In the progestogen-only pill, the hormones thicken the fluid in the womb, making it harder for sperm to reach the fallopian tubes. At the same time, they make the lining of the womb thinner, so a fertilized egg can't settle into it.

The pill is taken regularly, either every day, or for three weeks out of every four, and some types have to be taken at the same time every day. A doctor advises which type of pill is best for each person, and women on the pill must have regular health checks.

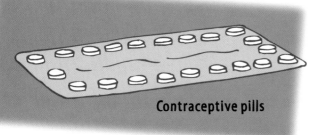

Contraceptive pills

Some women get side effects from taking the pill. They may put on weight, or get headaches, sore breasts, irregular periods, or high blood pressure. But the pill also has some good side effects. It can prevent painful periods and clear up acne. Sometimes the pill is given to girls just to help with these problems.

▶ INJECTIONS AND IMPLANTS

work with hormones in the same way as the pill. The main difference is that you don't have to remember to take a pill every day. A single injection in the bottom or arm lasts up to 12 weeks.

Implants are small soft tubes. A doctor or nurse inserts the tube under the skin in the upper arm. The implants last for about three years, slowly releasing the hormones into the body.

▶ THE IUS, OR INTRA-UTERINE

System, and IUD or Intra-Uterine Device are pushed up through the vagina and fitted inside the womb by a doctor or nurse.

The IUS is a small plastic T-shaped object that works by slowly releasing hormones, and lasts for about five years. It may cause sore breasts or pimples, but can make periods lighter.

The IUD (also called the coil) is T-shaped and made of plastic and copper. It doesn't use hormones, but stops sperm from getting to an egg and stops eggs from settling into the lining of the womb. It lasts for as long as ten years, but can cause heavy or painful periods.

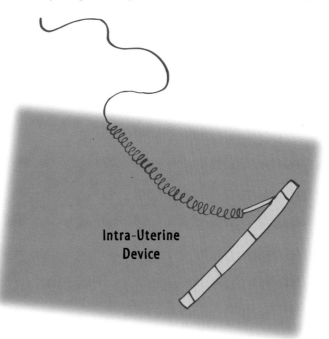

Intra-Uterine Device

IF DISASTER HAPPENS — a condom splits, a girl forgets to take her pill, neither partner take any precautions, or a girl is forced to have sex against her will — emergency contraception can prevent a possible pregnancy.

The emergency contraception pill (or morning-after pill) can be taken up to 72 hours (three days) after having intercourse, but it works best if taken within 24 hours. The longer you wait, the less effective it is. You can get emergency contraception pills free from a doctor, a family planning clinic, or a birth control center.

It is not possible to get emergency contraception for someone else, as the doctor or pharmacist will need to check that the pills are safe for the girl to take.

Emergency contraception is not meant to be taken on a regular basis. It is for emergencies only and it can't (and shouldn't) be taken twice in the same monthly period cycle without getting advice from a doctor.

Another form of emergency contraception is to have an IUD fitted within 120 hours (five days) of having intercourse (see previous page).

REMEMBER — NO METHOD OF CONTRACEPTION IS ABSOLUTELY RELIABLE. They only work when they are used properly *every* time. Mistakes can always happen.

OK, SO THAT'S enough about contraception, now what about STDs? Sexually transmitted diseases aren't new to the world. They've probably been around for as long as we have. The difference is that, to begin with anyway, no one knew what they were — and then when they did, no one wanted to talk about them.

People still don't like talking about STDs, or admitting they've got one. That's why they go on being passed from person to person.

Anyone can get an STD; it's not just poor people, or dirty people, or people who have sex a lot. Most STDs are passed from one person to another through sexual contact — touching an infected person's sexual organs or having sexual intercourse with him or her — but a few can be passed on in other ways.

And, of course, you can catch an STD even if you only have sexual contact with an infected person once. So don't think that you don't need to know about all this stuff, because you do.

REMEMBER!

The only way to avoid STDs is to use a CONDOM whenever you have any sexual contact with another person.

Any one of these people could have an STD! What a weird thought!

Oh, no! I'm going to die!

▶ **THERE ARE** a lot of different types of STDs — some of them are very serious and some of them are less so. Most can be cured, although some can permanently damage your health. A few STDs cannot be cured, and eventually they kill the people who have them.

The most common types of STDs are listed on the next few pages. The newest and, at present, the most dangerous of these is HIV/AIDS — see page 97.

▶ **YOU CAN'T ALWAYS** tell if you have an STD. With some types, the symptoms — the way it makes you feel — aren't always obvious. The only way to know for sure is to see a doctor. So even if you haven't had sexual contact with someone, if you ever have ANY kind of ache or pain in your belly or groin, any genital itching or rashes or stinging sensation when you pee, a very heavy or smelly discharge from your vagina or penis, unusual or extra-heavy periods, or notice anything unusual on or around your sexual organs — don't ignore it!

▶ **GET HELP.** Tell your parents or another adult, the school nurse, or see your doctor. It might well turn out to be nothing much at all, but if it is an STD it will need treatment.

There are also free special clinics that test for and treat STDs. Most are attached to local hospitals. You can find out where they are from the advice centers listed on pages 104–107, or try calling your local hospital.

Most important of all, if you do have an STD you must tell anyone you have had any sexual contact with, no matter HOW embarrassed you feel. If you can't tell them in person, then phone, text, or write to them. If you don't, they could become really sick or they could infect someone else!

Sorry I haven't seen you lately, but there's something you need to know ...

⊙ Chlamydia

This is an infection caused by bacteria (a type of germ). It is especially widespread among young men and women. One reason for this is that it can be hard to know you've got it as there are often no symptoms. Men can have a whitish discharge from the penis and/or find peeing painful. Women may have a heavier than normal discharge, and/or pain when they pee, abdominal pain, heavy periods, or bleeding between periods.

Chlamydia is spread by having intercourse with an infected person, or by touching the genitals of an infected person and then touching your own. It is cured by antibiotics, but if it is not treated, it can affect a woman's fertility (her ability to have children).

⊙ Genital herpes

There are two types of virus (another sort of germ) that cause genital herpes. One type causes blisters and sores around the mouth, nose, or eyes. The other causes blisters and sores around the genitals or anus.

Both are spread through sexual contact with an infected person, but can also be spread by kissing. There is no real cure for genital herpes. It can be treated with creams and pills that make the sores go away, but they can come back again.

⊙ Genital warts

These small growths appear in or around the genitals or the anus. They are caused by a virus, which is spread by sexual contact. They may itch or feel sore, or they may not hurt at all. They have to be removed, otherwise they spread quickly, and they can grow back again.

⊙ Nonspecific genital infections

These are all caused by bacteria. They include vaginitis (inflammation of the vagina), urethritis (inflammation of the urethra — the tube through the penis), cystitis (inflammation of the bladder — see page 96), and proctitis (inflammation of the rectum).

Not all of them are caught by sexual contact. The bacteria can develop for other reasons. It's possible to have an infection without knowing it, but they can cause discharges, red sores on the skin, or make it very painful to pee. They are all curable with antibiotics, but if left untreated can create problems later on with a man's testicles or a woman's fertility (her ability to have children).

PUBIC LICE (CRABS) & SCABIES

Not really STDs, but worth knowing about.

⊙ Pubic lice, or crabs

Not the same thing as head lice, these tiny insects cling to pubic or armpit hair. They are very hard to see, but they itch like crazy. You can catch them by close body or sexual contact, but also from the bedding or clothing of an infected person. They are treated with lotions.

⊙ Scabies

Caused by tiny insects, called mites, that live on our skin. Scabies can be caught by close body contact, but is more often picked up by contact with infected bedding or clothing. It is treated with creams or lotion.

ⓘ Gonorrhoea (or the clap)

This is a bacterial infection, like chlamydia. It has existed for thousands of years, and lately it's been on the increase again!

It is passed on through intercourse and oral sex. Men usually get a thickish discharge from their penis, may find peeing painful, and might feel like they've got a cold. Women often don't have any symptoms at all, but if they are pregnant they can pass the infection on to their baby. Gonorrhoea can also damage a man's testicles. It is cured with antibiotics.

ⓘ Syphilis (or the pox)

Another very ancient infection that once upon a time made people go blind, drove them mad, and eventually killed them. The symptoms are a painless sore on or near the vagina or penis, a rash on the body, and flu-like symptoms. Nowadays it can be cured with antibiotics and has become very rare in many countries.

ⓘ Hepatitis B Virus

Hepatitis A, B, and C all infect the liver (the organ that cleans poisons from your blood), but Hepatitis B is the only STD.

Hepatitis B is spread by sexual contact or by contact with infected blood or blood-stained saliva, for example by using dirty body piercing or tattooing tools, or reusing hypodermic syringes.

Hepatitis C is also spread by using dirty or infected tools or syringes, and Hepatitis A is spread by bad hygiene, such as not washing your hands after going to the toilet and then touching food or water.

People who get Hepatitis B may feel like they have the flu, or feel tired, lose their appetite, and look jaundiced — their skin and the whites of their eyes look yellow. There isn't really a cure for hepatitis, but with lots of care and rest most people do recover from it.

CANDIDIASIS (OR THRUSH) & CYSTITIS

These aren't exactly STDs either, but they are very widespread.

ⓘ Candidiasis (thrush) is a

fungus that lives on skin, and inside the mouth, vagina, and penis. Usually it's controlled by good bacteria in our bodies, but sometimes the fungus spreads.

This can be caused by taking antibiotics, by stress, wearing tight-fitting clothes a lot, over-using bubble baths or body sprays, and by having sex with someone who has thrush.

Thrush causes soreness and inflammation in the mouth, penis, or vagina, and/or itching, painful urinating, and a thick vaginal discharge. It is cured by using a special cream.

ⓘ Cystitis is an infection of

the bladder. It is very common, but is easily treated. It's caused by bacteria getting into the bladder, for example from bad hygiene (such as wiping from back to front after a poo, or not changing pads or tampons often enough), or from having intercourse.

The main symptoms are wanting to pee all the time, even though very little pee comes out, and a pain or burning feeling when you pee. It's cured by a taking a course of antibiotics. Drinking lots and lots of water helps, too.

⚠ HIV/AIDS

This STD is fairly new (it was first identified in the early 1980s), but it's spreading fast. Some of its symptoms are treatable, but so far there is NO CURE for it.

HIV stands for human immunodeficiency virus. This virus causes an illness known as AIDS, or acquired immune deficiency syndrome. Usually your body is very good at fighting off illnesses. It's able to do this because of something called your immune system. HIV attacks the immune system. There are medicines that can help delay the effects of HIV, but they cannot cure it, so eventually HIV weakens your body so much that you develop AIDS.

AIDS is really a group of illnesses that include loss of weight, fever, breathing problems, eyesight problems, difficulty thinking, weakness, and finally death. As with HIV, there are medicines that can help people fight AIDS, but it cannot be cured.

It is possible to have HIV for as long as 10 years or more without knowing it, and without developing AIDS. But almost everyone who has HIV does eventually get AIDS.

The only way to know for sure whether or not someone has HIV is to take a blood test. If the blood test shows that the virus is in someone's blood that person is said to be HIV positive, although they may seem to be perfectly healthy.

The HI virus can live only in a person's blood, semen, vaginal fluids, or breast milk. It cannot live outside the body, so you can't get it by normal bodily contact with an infected person, such as hugging or holding hands. You cannot get it by being in the same room as an infected person or by someone coughing or sneezing near you. Neither can you get it from using or touching everyday objects, and you

DON'T get it off toilet seats or from mosquito or flea bites.

YOU CAN get HIV by having unprotected intercourse with an infected person — sex without using a condom — or by having oral sex, or touching the semen, penis, vagina, or anus of an infected person.

You can also get HIV by using the same hypodermic syringes or needles as an infected person. And it is possible to catch HIV from dirty needles or tools used for body piercing and tattooing.

If someone is pregnant and has HIV, she can pass the virus on to her baby either before or during birth. She could also infect her baby through her breast milk.

AIDS is a huge problem all around the world. About 3 million people died of it in the year 2003, and millions more die every year.

REMEMBER
BE SURE, BE SAFE — EITHER AVOID HAVING CLOSE SEXUAL CONTACT WITH ANYONE, OR USE A CONDOM EVERY TIME!

Over 36 million people in the world are known to have HIV/AIDS at present – about 2.5 million of them are under 15.

▶ **AT THE BEGINNING** of this chapter, I said that your body is yours; you own it. This is true, but one of the saddest and hardest things in life we sometimes have to deal with is that not everyone respects or honors that fact.

Sexual needs or desires can cause some extraordinarily powerful emotions and there are some people who let their emotions make them behave in ways that are dangerous.

If these people are older, stronger, or more powerful in some way, they may use their power to make someone else do something sexual that he or she doesn't want to do. When someone does this to another person they are doing something WRONG — they are mistreating or sexually abusing that person.

LEAVE ME ALONE! GO AWAY! HELP!

Safety First!
Be streetwise — do your best to protect yourself from danger.

✖ Don't wander around on your own, especially after dark or in unfamiliar or badly lit places, such as alleyways, parks, parking lots, country roads, or woodlands.

✖ Don't take rides in cars or trucks with anyone unless your parents know about it. If you are out with your friends, stay with them — no matter what happens.

✖ Make sure your parents or another adult always know where you are going and when you expect to be back.

✖ Never give a stranger your name, phone number, or address, even over the Internet.

✖ Don't talk at all to strangers who approach you, even if they know your name.

✖ Never accept sweets, drinks, or medicines from a stranger.

✖ If someone is bothering you and you want them to stop, say so clearly and loudly. If they won't stop, shout or scream until they leave you alone — no matter who it is.

▶ **SEXUAL ABUSE** can be difficult to understand and very hard to talk about. Many people, especially adults, do not really want to believe that sexual abuse happens — but it does!

Sexual abuse might mean that someone tries to kiss you, touch you, or hold you in ways that you don't want them to. Or it might be someone trying to make you kiss, touch, or hold him or her in a way that you don't want to.

An abuser might try to talk about sexual things to you, or may try to scare or threaten you into doing something — or physically force you into doing it.

▶ **ALL FORMS OF** sexual abuse (including sexual harassment, such as sexual teasing, badgering, bullying, or threatening) are against the law.

If someone makes you have sexual intercourse of any kind when you don't want to, it is called **RAPE** and it is against the law.

Even if you've been on a date with someone or have been willingly kissing or touching that person, if you are forced to go any further than you want to go that is still rape or (if you don't actually have intercourse) attempted rape. And remember, even if you have agreed to sex, if you are below the age of consent (see page 85) the person you had sex with can still be charged with rape.

There are no excuses for rape — none. Not drugs, not drink, not overpowering emotions, not anything.

WHAT IS NOT SEXUAL ABUSE

It's not always easy to know if someone is abusing you. After all, sexual abusers don't all wear dirty raincoats. They don't even have to touch you — they can abuse you by talking to you in a sexual way or by showing you sexy pictures or films.

Not everyone who does want to touch you is going to be an abuser, either. The usual, natural, hugging and kissing that goes on in families and between friends is fine. You may not like being hugged by an elderly aunt or uncle, but this is not abuse.

Come and give your Auntie Myrtle a hug, then.

EEEK!!!

Neither is it abuse if you have hurt yourself and someone is trying to help you, such as a teacher, nurse, or doctor.

Abuse is when someone does or says something unusual, shocking, or frightening to you, something that you know they would not do in front of other people.

But even if you're not sure — if it bothers you, tell someone!

▶ **ONE OF THE** worst things about sexual abuse is than the abuser could be anyone — an older kid, a kid your age, or an adult. He or she could be a stranger or someone you know, such as a neighbor, a teacher, or youth club leader, a friend of the family, or even someone who is part of your family.

Being abused — especially if it is by someone you know and love — is deeply frightening. It can be so frightening, in fact, that kids who are abused often tell themselves that it must be THEIR fault, that somehow they must have done something wrong, otherwise it wouldn't have happened to them.

THIS IS NOT SO!

No matter what the situation is, or who the abuser is, or what they say — if you've been abused it is never your fault.

> You know, it's really your fault. If you hadn't behaved like that I wouldn't have done it.

> Hi, it's me. Listen, I'm sorry, but I really need to talk to someone ...

▶ **NO ONE SHOULD** ever ask you to keep a secret about abuse. If you are ever abused or you think you may have been, or you know someone who is being abused, you must tell an adult you trust — no matter how frightening, difficult, or embarrassing this may be. And you must do it right away!

If you cannot tell a parent, or someone else in your family, tell your teacher, your doctor, or a friend's parent — or phone one of the helplines or centers listed on pages 104–107.

Abuse of any kind is ALWAYS wrong, and all adults know this. If someone is guilty of abuse they must be stopped, no matter who they are — even if the abuser is someone you love. And anyone who has suffered from abuse needs to be comforted, cared for, and reassured that they are not to blame.

▶ **PART OF GROWING** up is learning how to take care of yourself — including taking care of your body. This doesn't only mean keeping yourself safe from an unwanted pregnancy or an STD, or protecting yourself from abuse. It also means keeping your body healthy.

➡ Think about the kinds of food and drink you are putting into it.

➡ Think what smoking, alcohol, or illegal drugs can do to it.

➡ Remember to get enough sleep.

➡ Remember to wash your body and hair regularly and clean your teeth twice a day.

➡ Remember to visit the dentist every six months.

➡ And if ever you are worried about your body or your health in any way — go to a doctor.

Come on now, this won't hurt ...

AARGH!

▶ **VISITING A DOCTOR** is something even adults sometimes have problems with. When you are a child, a parent or another adult makes the decision about where and when you go to the doctor. A trip to the doctor can be a disturbing event for a child, so we may grow up being nervous or frightened of doctors.

But doctors are there to help you. They won't judge you, or criticize you, and they will keep whatever you tell them private.

When you are 18, you can choose your own doctor and take responsibility for your own health care. This means that the doctor will not discuss your health, or any medication he or she gives you, with your parents or any other legal guardian unless you want them to.

Even if you are under 18, doctors do not have to tell your parents or guardian about your appointment or any treatment you may have — as long as they feel that you fully understand your situation and the treatment they are offering you.

No matter how you feel about your body, it deserves your care and respect.

Now this won't hurt, but it might feel a little strange!

▶ **WHEN YOU GO** to a new doctor for the first time, he or she may want to give you a general health check. This means taking your blood pressure (usually by putting a type of pressure bandage around your arm), and checking your heart, lungs, abdomen, eyes, mouth, height, and weight

▶ **IF YOU'RE A GIRL** and you are sexually active (having intercourse) and you want some form of contraception other than condoms, you may need a pelvic or internal examination. This means that a doctor will check the inside of your vagina and your cervix.

To do this, you have to lie on your back on an examination table, with your knees bent and legs apart. The doctor puts a long metal instrument called a speculum into your vagina to hold the vaginal walls apart. Then the doctor shines a flashlight

into your vagina so that she or he can check that everything looks okay.

To examine your womb and ovaries, the doctor takes the speculum out and puts the finger of one hand into your vagina and at the same time, uses the other hand to press down gently on your stomach.

A pelvic exam isn't painful, but it is, without doubt, a **completely weird** experience. There are all sorts of reasons why a pelvic exam may be necessary, so at some point in her life almost every girl or woman has one. And everyone finds them hugely embarrassing — at least the first time! Doctors understand this and usually do their best to help you relax.

Both male and female doctors do pelvic examinations, but it's perfectly okay to ask for a female doctor to do it, and/or for a nurse or your mom to be with you while you have one.

▶ **BOYS DON'T HAVE** pelvic examinations as such, but if they have any kind of problem with their penis or testicles the doctor may need to look at and possibly handle them.

In particular, he or she may gently press or push the area around the base of the testicles, near to where the prostate gland is.

Just as with girls, most boys find the thought of showing their most private parts to a doctor totally nerve-wracking. And many boys worry that if a doctor handles their penis, they may get an erection, even though sex is absolutely the last thing on their mind. But all doctors understand this and they, at least, are not embarrassed by it.

Try thinking of your body as a fabulously expensive car. If something goes wrong with a car it is taken to a garage for a check-up, otherwise it will eventually break down and stop working. If something goes wrong with your body, you need to take it to the doctor!

CHECK IT OUT
A doctor who has been specially trained to treat women — particularly anything to do with their sexual organs — is called a **gynecologist**.

▶ **AND FINALLY!**
Your body is the most amazing once-in-a-lifetime gift you will ever have. Male or female, tall or short, thin or fat, it's a spectacular, miraculous piece of machinery and it's all yours. Understand it, guard it, treat it well ... and wear it with pride!

USEFUL STUFF

▶ **IF YOU NEED** advice or information about something and you don't feel that you can ask anyone you know, there are a number of groups and organizations that may be able to help you.

Some of these organizations are publicly funded (they're given money by the government out of the taxes paid by people who are working). Others are funded by charities (paid for by gifts of money from people who support them).

They all offer confidential advice and information, and in some cases can give practical help or treatment as well. If you are not sure which organization is right for you, telephone first or go to their web site if they have one. Some phone lines can be pretty busy, so if you don't get through the first time, keep trying — and check out the "Telephone Tips" in the box below.

▶ **THE ORGANIZATIONS** and web sites listed here are just some of those that are available. Some may have a local branch in your area or, if they can't help you, they should be able to put you in touch with a group that can.

TELEPHONE TIPS

Getting information over the phone can be tough at the best of times, let alone when you've got a problem to solve.

→ Think carefully about what you want to know. Make a short list of your key questions before you call, and don't try to explain too much at first.

→ If you are using a public pay phone, make sure you have plenty of change. It may take a while to get to the right person.

→ Have a pen and paper with you to take down notes.

→ The first person you speak to may be a receptionist. Ask to speak to someone who can help you with … and name your problem. The receptionist will either put you through to someone who can answer your questions, or may give you the phone number of a different organization to call.

→ Explain your question or problem as clearly and simply as you can.

→ Be prepared to answer questions about yourself and your situation, but if you are not sure what you are being asked, or why, don't be afraid to ask for an explanation.

→ Tell the truth. It won't help you if you give out the wrong information.

CHECK IT OUT

In the U.S. — calls made to telephone numbers beginning with 800 and 888 are free.

ADOPTION:

✱ BIRTHMOTHER.COM   Free online support group and resource center for women and men considering adoption of their unborn child.
www.birthmother.adoption.com

✱ NATIONAL ADOPTION INFORMATION CLEARINGHOUSE (NAIC)   An information clearinghouse on all aspects of adoption.
P.O. Box 1182
Washington, D.C. 20013-1182
888-251-0075
www.calib.com/naic

CONTRACEPTION, SEX, STDs, PREGNANCY, ABORTION:

✱ ADVOCATES FOR YOUTH   Fights for young people's rights to realistic sex education, family planning, and effective HIV/STD prevention programs.
2000 M Street NW
Suite 750
Washington, D.C. 20036
www.advocatesforyouth.org

✱ AMERICAN SOCIAL HEALTH ASSOCIATION (ASHA)   Through network of public and private health providers, ASHA provides facts, support, and resources to find referrals and get information about sexually transmitted diseases.
P.O. Box 13827
Research Triangle Park, NC 27709
www.ashastd.org

✱ CDC NATIONAL AIDS HOTLINE
1-800-342-7889

✱ GO ASK ALICE!   The health question and answer Internet service provided by Columbia University's Health Education Program. The service reads and answers letters from high school and college students on sexuality, health, and drugs, among many other health topics.
www.goaskalice.com

✱ PRO-CHOICE RESOURCES   Provides accurate health-related information on risks and consequences surrounding sexual activity. Includes information on birth control, STDs, abortion, adoption, and parenting.
32-49 Hennepin Avenue South, Suite 255
Minneapolis, MN 55408
888-439-0124
www.birdsandbees.org

✱ PLANNED PARENTHOOD   Provides reproductive health care, free or at reduced cost, in clinics across the country. The web site has links to local clinics.
434 West 33rd Street
New York, NY 10001
1-800-230-PLAN
www.plannedparenthood.com

✱ SCARLETEEN   Web site contains information about contraception, STDs, relationships, diverse sexual orientation, and numbers for various hot lines.
www.scarleteen.com

✱ SEX, ETC.   A teen-produced web site that answers questions about sex, contraception, STDs, sexual orientation, abortion, adoption, teen parenting, and more.
www.sxetc.com

➡

GAY AND LESBIAN:

✴ YOUTH GUARDIAN SERVICES   Youth-run nonprofit organization that provides services for gay, lesbian, bisexual, transgendered, questioning, and straight youth.
Youth Guardian Services, Inc.
101 E. State Street #299
Ithaca, NY 14850
1-877-270-5152 (information line)
www.youth-guard.org

✴ YOUTHRESOURCE   Web site for gay, lesbian, bixsexual, transgender, and questioning young people 13–24 years old. Offers support, resources, and peer-to-peer education. The site is a project of Advocates for Youth.
www.youthresource.com

GENERAL ADVICE

✴ ABOUT.COM   Web site provides advice on all aspects of teen life, including sex, health, dating, depression, and self-esteem.
www.about.com/teens

✴ HEALTHYPLACE   Web site providing mental health information and support.
www.healthyplace.com

✴ NATIONAL CENTER FOR AT-RISK YOUTH
Provides over-the-phone counseling, crisis intervention, and referrals for teens dealing with difficult life situations. Operates a national call center for at-risk-youth, 800-USA-KIDS.
18750 Oxnard Street
Suite 412
Tarzana, CA 91356
www.thursdayschild.org

✴ TEENGROWTH   Interactive web site dedicated to the health interests and well-being of the teen population. Offers information on alcohol, drugs, emotions, health, family, friends, school, and sex.
www.teengrowth.com

IN CANADA...

✴ ADOPTION COUNCIL OF CANADA   The umbrella organization for adoption in Canada, the council provides information and referrals in answer to adoption inquiries.
211 Bronson Avenue, #210
Ottawa, ON K1R 6H5
1-888-54-ADOPT
www.adoption.ca

✴ CANADA ADOPTS   Online resource providing information on private and public adoption agencies throughout Canada.
www.canadaadopts.com

✴ LESBIAN GAY BI YOUTH LINE   Service provided for youth by youth that provides confidential peer support through telephone listening, information,

and referral services. Its goal is to support the lesbian, gay, bisexual, transgendered, and questioning youth of Ontario.
1-800-268-YOUTH
www.youthline.ca

✳ PLANNED PARENTHOOD OF CANADA
Volunteer organization providing health care and information on reproductive and sexual health. Medical care related to reproductive health is available at clinics throughout Cananda.
1 Nicholas Street
Suite 430
Ottowa, ON K1N 7B7
www.ppfc.ca

✳ SPIDERBYTES.CA   Web site is a service of the Teen Sex Information Program of Planned Parenthood of Toronto. It responds to questions about sexual health issues and provides current information, links, and referral on topics relating to healthy sexuality.
www.spiderbytes.ca

✳ TEEN HEALTH   Provides access to health and medical information on a wide variety of topics.
Teen help line: 1-800-420-8336
www.chebucto.ns.ca/health/teenhealth

WORLD WIDE WEB SITES
All of these web sites contain loads of information about many of the topics covered in this book.

❑ **www.iwannaknow.org** — information and FAQs on teen sexual health and STDs from the American Social Health Association.

❑ **www.kidshealth.org** OR **www.teenshealth.org** — lots of information, FAQs, animations, and games. Operated by The Nemours Foundation, USA.

❑ **www.lifebytes.gov.uk** — for 11-14 year olds on all kinds of health stuff, including alcohol, drugs, eating, safety, and sex, from the UK's Health Education Authority.

❑ **www.likeitis.org.uk** — for 11-15 year olds on sex, contraception, periods, etc. Operated by Marie Stopes International.

❑ **www.somazone.com.au** — a Q&A website on relationships, sex, emotions, health, drugs, and more, from the Australian Drug Foundation.

❑ **www.teenwire.com** — FAQs, info, and fun stuff on sex and puberty, from the Planned Parenthood Federation of America.

❑ **www.thehormonefactory.com** — slow to load but lots of fun info for 10-12 year olds on sex and puberty from the Australian Research Centre in Sex, Health & Society.

GLOSSARY

▶ Words in small capitals, LIKE THIS, have their own entry.

abortion bringing a PREGNANCY to an end, by taking a special pill or by having an operation.

abuse when someone physically, sexually, or emotionally hurts or mistreats you.

acne groups of red, inflamed pimples on the face, chest, shoulders, or back. Often appears during puberty.

anus opening at the end of the RECTUM.

bacteria microscopic life forms. Some are harmful to us and some keep us healthy — see also CELLS.

birth control methods of CONTRACEPTION.

bisexual a person who is sexually attracted to males and females.

bladder a bag-like organ that collects urine.

blow job putting your partner's penis into your mouth.

cells the smallest units of life. All living things are made of cells. Some, such as BACTERIA, may have just one cell. Others, like us, have millions of cells.

circumcision an operation to remove the foreskin from a penis.

condom a method of CONTRACEPTION, which also protects the wearer from catching an STD.

contraception preventing PREGNANCY, by natural methods or by using drugs or devices.

discharge any clear, milky, or discolored liquid leaving the vagina or penis, other than blood, semen, or urine. Can sometimes indicate an infection. See also VAGINAL DISCHARGE.

Parts of the male SEX ORGANS:
epididymis
foreskin
glans
penis
prostate gland
scrotum
seminal vesicles
testicles
vas deferens

See diagram on page 19

ejaculation when semen squirts out of the penis — also known as coming.

embryo the stage of a baby's development inside the womb, from FERTILIZATION until about the eighth week of PREGNANCY.

erection when blood rushes into a penis so that it enlarges and gets stiff.

erogenous zones parts of the body that make you feel sexually excited when they are touched or stroked.

estrogen a female sex HORMONE.

fertilization when male SPERM cells enter and join up with female OVA or egg cells.

fetus the stage of a baby's development in the womb from about the eighth week of PREGNANCY until birth.

foreplay sexual stimulation that takes place usually (but not only) before INTERCOURSE.

gay a person who is a HOMOSEXUAL.

gender your sex — either male or female.

genitals the outer SEX ORGANS.

glands organs in the body that produce chemicals that carry out particular functions. For example, sweat glands produce sweat to keep our bodies cool.

heterosexual someone who is sexually attracted to people of the opposite sex.

HIV/AIDS a SEXUALLY TRANSMITTED DISEASE that attacks the immune system (the body's ability to fight off illness).

homosexual someone who is sexually attracted to people of the same sex.

hormones special chemicals released into the bloodstream by some GLANDS in order to act on a particular part of the body.

hymen a thin sheet of skin covering the vaginal opening.

intercourse having sex. Putting a penis inside a vagina.

lesbian a female HOMOSEXUAL.

masturbation touching or rubbing your SEXUAL ORGANS for pleasure.

Parts of the female SEX ORGANS:
cervix
clitoris
fallopian tubes
labia
ovaries
uterus (womb)
vagina
vaginal opening
vulva

See diagrams on pages 37 and 45

menopause when a woman's ovaries stop producing eggs and her PERIODS no longer happen.

monthly cycle the number of days from the start of one PERIOD to the beginning of the next.

natural method — see RHYTHM METHOD.

oral sex using your mouth and tongue to stimulate your partner's SEX ORGANS — see also BLOW JOB.

orgasm also called coming — a huge rush of pleasure achieved by sexual stimulation. Men usually (but not always) EJACULATE when they have an orgasm.

ova egg CELLS made in a woman's ovaries.

periods the monthly bleeding that women have when the womb lining and unfertilized egg are released from their body.

pregnancy the growth of a baby from a FERTILIZED egg inside the mother's womb. It lasts for roughly 40 weeks.

premenstrual syndrome (PMS) or premenstrual tension (PMT). The emotional upheaval many women go through just before or during the beginning of a PERIOD.

progesterone a female sex HORMONE.

pubic hair hair that grows around the external SEX ORGANS.

rape being forced to have INTERCOURSE against your will.

rectum the organ in the body that stores feces or waste matter.

rhythm method a type of CONTRACEPTION that relies on working out which days each month a woman is not producing an egg.

semen a milky liquid produced in the male SEX ORGANS to carry SPERM.

sex organs the parts of the body necessary for reproduction — making babies.

sexuality our attitude to sex — how we feel about it and the ways in which we are attracted to other people.

sexually transmitted diseasea (STDs) diseases or infections passed on by sexual INTERCOURSE or close body contact. (See pages 95–97 for a list of individual STDs.)

sperm the male sex CELL produced in the testicles.

spermicide a cream or gel used with contraceptives to kill SPERM.

straight a person who is a HETEROSEXUAL.

testosterone a male sex HORMONE.

toxic shock syndrome a bacterial infection that can be caused by infected wounds, or by wearing a tampon for too long.

urethra a tube from the BLADDER to the penis in men and urethral opening in women, by which urine leaves the body.

vaginal discharge a normally clear or milky liquid that helps to keep the vagina healthy.

virgin any male or female who has not had sexual INTERCOURSE.

wet dreams EJACULATING in your sleep.

withdrawal method taking the penis out of the vagina before EJACULATION.

INDEX